FAITH UNDER FIRE

Living with the Latter-day Saints

•Carol Avery Forseth•

Denver, Colorado

Unless otherwise noted, Scripture quotations are taken from the *New American Standard Bible* (c) The Lockman Foundation 1960, 1962, 1963, 1968, 1971, 1972, 1973, 1975, 1977. Used with permission. Other Scripture references, as noted, are from the *King James Version* of the Bible.

Names of Mormons have been changed to protect their privacy.

A division of Accent Publications, Inc.
12100 West Sixth Avenue
P.O. Box 15337
Denver, Colorado 80215

Copyright © 1989 Accent Publications, Inc.
Printed in the United States of America

All rights reserved. No portion of this book may be reproduced in any form without the written permission of the publishers, with the exception of brief excerpts in magazine reviews.

Library of Congress Catalog Card Number 88-83417

ISBN 0-89636-250-7

Acknowledgments

I'd like to thank a few people who have helped me with this book. First, there was Javier Trevino, who came along and asked me "How's the book coming?" every time I was ready to give up and throw it away. Then Jim Sthay, who faithfully read the rough draft and helped me think of titles. And the Mark Morris family, who loaned me their computer so I could type and revise the manuscript. Also, I'd like to thank Ron Forseth, who read every word aloud so I could hear how it sounded. He did that as a favor to a new friend who shared his interest in Mormonism. But now I'm even more thankful for Ron who, on December 18, 1988, became my husband.

Preface

I didn't go to Brigham Young University as a missionary—I went as a foolish student. At BYU, I learned about Mormonism, but I also learned about the God of the Bible.

So why have I written this book? Because from a membership of six people in 1830, the Mormon Church reached its first million members in 1947, its second in 1963, its third in 1971, its fourth in 1978, its fifth in 1982, in April 1986, the Mormon church baptized its six millionth member and as of December 31, 1988 the membership stands at 6,650,000! The Church of Jesus Christ of Latter-day Saints has tripled in size during the past 25 years. Mormon Church membership in Texas and Georgia doubles every 10 years. In Texas and Georgia? In the Bible Belt?

Christians don't understand what Mormonism is really about. Americans in general, with a dimming sense of Christian influences, do not know what Mormonism is really about. Mormons reject religious pluralism. Their ultimate goal is to supersede, or replace, other religions. The Mormon Church leaders manage their public image well, so we don't hear much about their growing power and influence. But we cannot afford to ignore such a rising, authoritarian, powerful church.

This book is not an attack against the integrity, character, or intelligence of the Latter-day Saint people. In fact, I count many as my friends. I have tried to write as objectively, honestly, and kindly as I could. If I have been successful, the reader will know that this book is not anti-Mormon sensationalism. But it is an inside look at Mormonism. Ninety-seven percent of the students at Brigham Young University are Mormons—and BYU is the very heart of the Church.

I examine Mormonism in light of the Bible. As a Christian, my only authority on religious doctrine is the Bible, and I evaluate this, and any, religious system by comparing its teachings with the Bible.

Are Mormons Christians? What *is* a Christian? The Mormon church leaders and members now describe themselves as Christians, although in their earlier days, they didn't want to be identified with Christians. The official name of the church is the Church of Jesus Christ of Latter-day Saints. Mormons sing about Jesus and pray in Jesus' name. But a Christian, according to the Bible, is an individual who has faith in Christ through repentance from sin. It is someone who knows Jesus Christ personally. Joining any church does not make a person a Christian. Some people know Christ as a result of their church's teachings and others in spite of them. There may be some true Christians in the Mormon Church, but Mormon doctrine does not lead people to a saving knowledge of Christ.

I hope this inside, honest look at this cult through my experiences on the campus at BYU will give you deeper insight, greater awareness, and a heightened realism toward witnessing to those who are members of the Mormon Church.

Notes:
[1] *The 1989-1990 Church Almanac.* Salt Lake City: Deseret News, 1988
[2] Heinerman, John, and Shupe, Anson, *The Mormon Corporate Empire.* Boston: Beacon Press, 1985, page 81.

Chapter One

I was tired. Tired of talking with college recruiters, tired of accepting brochures, tired of wandering from building to building in the Phoenix heat. After a long afternoon at the High School Senior's Fair I decided to head for home.

Then one last sign caught my eye. Brigham Young University, Provo, Utah. I knew the name—an acquaintance had attended BYU. Pausing for a moment, I peeked in the doorway and was welcomed inside by a clean-cut young man wearing a sport coat and tie.

"How do you do? My name is Roger Smith. And you are. . . ?"

"Carol Avery."

"It's a pleasure to meet you. What do you know about Brigham Young University?"

"Nothing. In fact, I was just passing by on my way home and happened to look in."

"I'd like to tell you about our school," he said. "First, let me give you a pamphlet about BYU to read at your convenience. . .oh, I see you have several already."

"I've talked with quite a few recruiters this afternoon."

"You must be tired. Why don't you sit down and watch this short movie about BYU?"

I relaxed in a chair, glad for the ten minute respite. The film explained that Brigham Young University, with an enrollment of more than 25,000 students, was supported and operated by the Church of Jesus Christ of Latter-day Saints—the Mormons. The school was named for the Mormon pioneer, Brigham Young, who led the Mormons to Utah in the mid-1800s. Nearly every field of study was offered at the "the Y," as I heard the students call their school. The campus was situated in a beautiful mountain valley in northern Utah. After watching the movie, I was willing to learn more about BYU.

"I'm going to be studying music. I play the French horn," I mentioned. "What can you tell me about the music department?"

"How interesting. I studied music also—and I play horn as well. The department is outstanding, and the faculty members are known across the nation."

"I'm not Mormon," I confessed. "Am I still eligible to attend Brigham Young University?"

"Certainly. We accept any qualified student as long as he or she agrees to abide by the standards of the University and the Church. We request that students refrain from use of tobacco, alcoholic beverages, and hallucinatory drugs. There's a copy of the Code of Honor in the material I gave you. Although most of our students are Latter-day Saints, students of all religions attend BYU.

"I must tell you that tuition rates are slightly higher for non-LDS students because the Mormon Church finances seventy percent of the University budget. Church members have contributed through tithing all their lives, but the rates you pay as a non-Mormon are still lower than any other private institution."

Mr. Smith handed me an information card to fill out. "If your grades are good, you ought to apply for a scholarship. I don't usually give away catalogs, but I do have some in my car. If you are interested, I'd like you to have one." He left the room, returning as I completed the information card.

"Here is the catalog and my business card," he said. "Please contact me if you need any help. I hope you consider attending Brigham Young University. It's been a pleasure talking with you."

That evening I sat down to sort out my brochures and my thoughts. While poring over the material from Mr. Smith, I found the Code of Honor that all students sign before entering the University. According to the Code, all students were to abide by the standards of the Church of Jesus Christ of Latter-day Saints, to be honest, to respect personal and property rights, and to obey the law. Students also agreed to comply with all University regulations, to observe the *Word of Wisdom* (abstinence from coffee, tea, tobacco, alcohol, and hallucinatory drugs), and to live the law of chastity. They were to observe high standards of taste and decency in dress, and were to help others fulfill their responsibilities under the Honor Code.

I also found a dress code that set the standard for men's hair length and women's dress lengths. Women were allowed to wear dress pants, but no one wore "grubbies" on campus.

I began to wonder about the Mormon Church. I could count on one hand all the Latter-day Saints I knew, and all of them were exemplary people. I knew nothing of and cared little about their doctrine, but I had heard of the Mormon Tabernacle Choir, the Mormons' emphasis on family life, and their missionary zeal. I had never cared much about religious doctrines, and I supposed that as long as the people were friendly and the rules weren't too strict, beliefs mattered little. God and church and religion were not for me, a contemporary American high school senior.

The following week, during a Phoenix Youth Symphony rehearsal, I remembered that my friend Sharon Stern, the principal horn player, was a Mormon. We had shared a hotel room during a music convention, and I remembered seeing her read some "Mormon book." During a break, I told her of my new interest in Brigham Young University.

Sharon clapped her hands in delight. "Guess what!" she said. "I've already sent my application to BYU. I hope you decide to go there, too."

"Well," I was quick to add, "I don't know much about it yet. What can you tell me about BYU?"

"It's beautiful. I've been there before. The music department is great and the horn teacher is outstanding. He's the first chair player in the Utah Symphony." A questioning look crossed Sharon's face. "You're not Mormon, are you? What sect do you belong to?"

I hesitated, and then asked, "Sect? It's hard to say. I don't attend church much. I'm just a Christian, I suppose."

"Oh, that's okay," Sharon answered. "Mormons are Christians, too. You know, the real name of our church is The Church of Jesus Christ of Latter-Day Saints. Did you know that I used to be a Methodist?"

I shook my head as she continued. "About four years ago I joined the Church, and it answered a lot of questions I had. If you come to BYU, you'll have a chance to see what it's all about."

That night I told my parents about my conversation with Sharon.

"Brigham Young?" asked my mother. "They say it's a good school. The academic and moral standards are high. Why don't you make an appointment to see Mr. Bradford at school? High school counselors have applications and lots of information about colleges."

When I went to see Mr. Bradford in the counseling office he said, "Brigham Young University? I earned my master's degree there. I'd be more than happy to write you a recommendation. I have applications here for admission and for scholarships."

I decided to complete and send in the forms. "Why not?" I told myself. "Everyone says BYU is wonderful. I like adventure. Utah is a beautiful state. It's almost December, and I need to make up my mind soon about where to attend college."

After putting the forms in the mail I was relieved. It felt good to take some action instead of waiting and wondering. "After all," I told myself, "what do I have to lose?"

The Christmas season was upon us, and my thoughts of Christmas shopping replaced my dreams of college. This year, my 15-year-old sister, Nancy, caused a disturbance in our family by visiting a Baptist church. She was, in my father's words, "getting churchy." My two brothers were irritated, but I didn't care, as long as she would keep her religion to herself.

Then Mom announced that the family was going to visit church with Nancy to show our broad-minded support. On Sunday Mom, Dad, and all four kids grudgingly piled into the car to go see what the "Bible bangers" were like. We weren't disappointed. The Baptists were reading the Bible just as we expected.

During the offering, I picked one up and casually flipped through it. At the top of one page I read, "He, your Teacher will no longer hide Himself, but your eyes will behold your Teacher. And your ears will hear a word behind you, 'This is the way, walk in it,' whenever you turn to the right or to the left" (Isaiah 30:20-21).

"Hey," I thought, "That sounds good. I wouldn't mind hearing a voice behind me telling me where to go to school next year. I wonder if God would do that?" I dismissed the thought, but Nancy continued attending church which, for some reason, irritated me. I began to feel like a heathen just because I didn't want to go to church, even though I did go again to keep peace in the family.

Between Mormonism and the Baptist church, religion had suddenly become an important matter. I had never before been forced to take a stand for or against any religion. I imagined God up in the sky somewhere, minding His own business while I minded mine. I supposed that as long as I made good use of the talents He gave me, and tried to become a better person, God would surely be pleased, even if I weren't the pious type. But that Baptist preacher kept talking about salvation and receiving Christ—and I occasionally wondered about "hearing a voice behind me."

One evening my sister came home after a prayer meeting saying she had accepted Christ and was going to be baptized. And I did see a change. Something was different about Nancy as I watched her closely throughout the week. By the next Sunday, I still hadn't figured her out. The rest of the family, also intrigued by Nancy's attitude, decided to attend her church one more time. "Not I!" I exclaimed. "I've had enough religion to last me 'til my old age."

Everyone left and I wandered the empty house all morning, trying to push religion out of my mind. Instead, Christ and my response to Him filled my troubled thoughts. I was unprepared for the exuberance of my parents and my brothers as they marched triumphantly into the house after church.

"Guess what, Carol!" said my mother. She had tears in her eyes and even my older brother was beaming. "We accepted Christ into our lives, each of us, this morning. They gave an invitation, and we each decided to commit our lives to Christ." She told the story in detail, and said the family was returning in the evening to talk with the pastor about baptism.

Suddenly my face felt hot and the tears began to fall. No longer was I merely avoiding religion—I was rejecting Christ. All this time I'd thought God was impersonal, and now I realized just how personal He was. Jesus died in *my* place, and offered *me* a new life. Would I take it, or leave it? That afternoon I had to face the questions honestly, and I knew there was only one response.

"Yes, Jesus," I said in my awkward, unaccustomed way, "you're right. How, where, when could I choose against you? If you'll take me as I am, I'll give my life to you."

I joined the family that night as we talked to the pastor, and we were baptized together as Christians and new members of the North Phoenix Baptist Church.

I noticed immediate changes in my attitude. Returning to high school after Christmas, I felt a real love and compassion for people—strangers, friends, even those individuals who usually irked me. To my surprise, many of my classmates said they noticed a different air about me.

My family was similarly transformed. Never before had my father, a mortician by profession, returned from a day's work whistling and smiling. Sibling rivalry didn't disappear entirely, but we began to handle conflicts more gently.

I began to wonder, after God changed my life, whether I ought to attend BYU. All I knew to do was pray that He would help me know His will. I asked other Christians what they thought about it.

"Carol!" said my Sunday School teacher, "surely you're not serious! I think you'd better study up before you think of going to Brigham Young. They'd probably convert you to Mormonism. Don't forget you're just a new believer."

I was distressed and confused. "Lord," I prayed, "I really want to do your will, but I'm afraid I won't recognize it. Please help me know what to do."

Every week at orchestra rehearsal, Sharon shared her enthusiasm with me. We both were struck by the adult idea of going off to college. Sharon was sure I would love BYU. If I went, she promised, we would be roommates in the dormitory. One night she said, "Carol, next week our ward is having an open house and dinner. We are supposed to bring guests. Would you and your family like to attend?"

"Your ward?" I asked.

"Yes. Our church is divided into wards, which are the same as your church congregations. And several wards together form a stake. That's how the Church is organized."

I wanted to learn more about the LDS Church, and my family, still broad-minded, decided to join me, so we met Sharon and her family at the ward chapel. Entering the building, we found ourselves in a large gymnasium set with tables and a potluck supper.

As we waited for dinner, Sharon introduced me to her bishop, the spiritual leader of the ward. She explained that Mormon bishops are unsalaried church members who hold full-time jobs while serving three-year leadership terms.

After a delicious meal, we watched a short movie called "Meet the Mormons" and then joined a lecture tour group

Living with the Latter-day Saints

led by two young men dressed in black suits, ties, and white shirts. One directed us to a series of large pictures along a hallway.

He switched on a light under the first picture—a nineteenth-century portrait of a young man. "I would like to begin by sharing with you the testimony of Joseph Smith, whom our Heavenly Father sent to restore Christ's Church on the earth in the latter days," said one of the men. "He was born in 1805. At the age of fifteen he was in Palmyra, New York during a period of religious revival. Many churches wanted Joseph to join, and Joseph became confused. One day, in his Bible, he read chapter one, verse five of the epistle of James: 'If any of you lack wisdom, let him ask of God, that giveth to all men liberally and upbraideth not; and it shall be given him' (KJV)."

The men, Mormon missionaries, moved ahead to a painting of Joseph Smith kneeling in a forest. "Joseph went into the woods to ask God for this wisdom. As he knelt, a pillar of light appeared and descended upon him. Suddenly he saw two personages standing before him. One spoke, saying, 'This is my beloved Son. Hear Him!' These two personages were our Heavenly Father and His Son Jesus Christ.

"Joseph was startled by this vision, but he asked the personages which church was right, and which he should join. They answered that he was to join none of them, for they were all wrong, and taught the doctrines of men and not of God."

Our guide moved to a new picture. "The personages disappeared, and Joseph was left to ponder these glorious things for three years. When he told other people about the vision, they criticized and ridiculed him, but he remained true to what he had seen. Then one night, as

Joseph prayed at his bedside, an angel of light appeared. The angel introduced himself as a messenger of God named Moroni, and said he came to tell Joseph of a book written on golden plates that were hidden in the Hill Cumorah near Joseph's home. The book was written by prophets of an ancient American civilization. It contained the account of these former inhabitants of the American continent, and the revelations they received from the Lord. The plates also told the story of Jesus Christ's visit to the Americas.

"The angel Moroni told Joseph to extract and translate the plates with the help of two special seer's stones, called the Urim and Thummim. Joseph found the plates, just as Moroni had said, and completed the task of translating them into the Book of Mormon. This book was first published in 1830. We accept this revelation as a divine and sacred Scripture along with the Bible."

The missionary motioned us ahead, and his companion continued the speech. "While they translated the Book of Mormon, Joseph Smith and his scribe, Oliver Cowdery, constantly sought divine inspiration. Once, while they were in the woods praying, Peter, James, and John, three of the original apostles, now resurrected, appeared. The came to bestow upon Joseph and Oliver an important power and authority—the very same priesthood that the original apostles had received from Christ. The apostles gave them the authority to restore upon the earth the true Church, which had been lost after the last apostle died.

"These resurrected apostles told Joseph Smith to organize the Church again. As in Jesus' day, it was to be directed by apostles and prophets who received revelation from the risen Christ. Joseph did as he was commanded and established the Church of Jesus Christ of Latter-day

Living with the Latter-day Saints

Saints. Today we are still guided by apostles and a prophet who receive revelations from Christ."

He continued, turning on a light under a painting of thirteen dignified, elderly men. "Jesus Christ is the head of our Church, and He directs it through revelation to His prophets. When Joseph Smith, the first Latter-day prophet, died, the Lord called another to fill his place. Since that time a living prophet has always been on earth to teach the members of the Church what the Lord would have them do. This is today's Prophet and his Twelve Apostles.

"Today our Church is led by Spencer W. Kimball,[1] a true prophet. We know that the Lord reveals to him the things that are vital to our salvation. When we follow his counsel, we can be assured of blessings from the Lord."

The first missionary spoke again. "This concludes our formal presentation. I want to bear testimony to you of the truth of these things. I know God lives, that Jesus is the Christ, and that they are separate beings of flesh and bone. I testify that these two did come to earth and appear to Joseph Smith and that this is the true Church. I say these things in the name of Jesus Christ, Amen."

The group dispersed. As Sharon escorted us toward the exit, my sister peeked into a room with a curtain drawn across the front. "Is that the stage?" she asked.

"Oh, no," Sharon replied with a laugh, "that is the baptistry. We baptize all new members. The Church is growing fast."

I lay awake that night, staring into the darkness and pondering all I had seen and heard. Without a doubt, I noted, the Mormons were efficient. The building was clean and new, the food was delicious, the members were friendly, and the tour was well-organized. It was as though I'd visited a well-run corporation.

Yet, I was troubled by the missionaries' lecture. They said all churches except their own were false. They said nothing about a personal relationship with Christ. Instead they spoke of angels of light, present-day prophets, and new Scriptures. I was a beginner at Bible study—maybe everything they said was in the Bible somewhere. I hadn't read the whole Bible yet. But I hadn't found Jesus through an angel or a prophet or new Scriptures.

So what was I to do? I wanted to attend BYU, but what about the Mormon religion? I would learn a lot, maybe even more than I wanted to know. But maybe the Mormon influence wouldn't be too strong. Maybe I'd meet some Christians. Once again I turned to Jesus, my new friend and counselor. "Help me know, Lord," I prayed. "Please don't let me go astray."

A week later I was offered a four-year full-tuition scholarship to BYU. I accepted it.

I was also accepted into the BYU honors program, which offered a seminar for entering freshmen before registration. I decided to take advantage of the opportunity to meet people and get oriented to the University. The summer slipped away, and sooner than I expected or even hoped, it was time to prepare for college.

The night before I left, Mom and I had a heart-to-heart talk.

"Carol," she said, "we're going to miss you. We've tried to bring you up to be a sensible girl, and now we can only pray that God will guide you. You may be pressured by those Mormons, and I want you to know that whatever you do we're behind you."

"Oh, Mom," I exclaimed. "I'm not going to become a Mormon. I wouldn't give up my new relationship with

Living with the Latter-day Saints

Jesus Christ for anything."

"Yes, I know," she answered. "I just want you to know that we love you, no matter what. And remember, you don't have to stay there if you are terribly unhappy. Don't keep suffering if it's not right. Call us collect if you ever need anything. But most important, stay close to Jesus. He's going to take care of you."

I went to bed early, anticipating the long drive ahead to Provo, Utah. And I realized, as I dropped off to sleep, that the next day I would enter a whole new world.

Note:
[1] Spencer W. Kimball passed away in 1985. On November 19, 1985, Ezra Taft Benson was set apart as the new president and prophet of the Church of Jesus Christ of Latter-day Saints.

Chapter Two

The morning was still and cool as we rose to pack the car. My father and I hugged Mom, and we backed out of the driveway. I turned for a last look at home and watched Mom waving frantically until she could no longer see us.

I wondered what lay ahead. I had to admit I was afraid. I forced myself to think about the words of Isaiah 43:2: "When you pass through the waters, I will be with you. . .when you walk through the fire, you will not be scorched, nor will the flame burn you. For I am the Lord your God."

"But Lord," I thought, "walking through fire will be scary, even with you by my side." Maybe I should back out. Had I passed the point of no return? I kept my thoughts to myself, and we kept driving.

The day's travel ended at a motel just outside Provo. The next morning, we explored the town. When we checked the phonebook, we found a listing for the First Baptist Church. We stopped by, but the church was dark and locked. Peering in the windows, I saw an auditorium with only fifteen or twenty rows of pews. "Looks small," I said to my dad. "I've never attended a church this small before."

We found our way to campus, parked the car, and began to explore the "Y" on foot. The weather was clear and breezy, and the bright sunshine made even the grass sparkle. Never had I seen a school with such well-kept grounds and buildings. There was no graffiti or even litter in sight. Fountains and gardens adorned the walkways.

We entered the Harris Fine Arts Center, the home of the music department. The door opened onto the second floor of a three-level art gallery with concert and theater halls in each corner. As we walked down an open staircase, we were awed by the grandeur of the building. We wandered down to the ground floor and found hallways of music practice rooms.

Over lunch Dad taught me how to write checks and balance my new checking account, and we returned to campus for seminar registration. I received my room key, and we hauled my belongings to the seventh floor of the Deseret Towers dormitory. Now I was sure I had passed the point of no return. When we finished, I walked down to the car to see my father off.

"God bless you," he said as he hugged me fiercely. "Take care of yourself. We'll be praying for you." It sounded trite, but we were both short of words.

"See you at Christmas."

I couldn't say good-bye—I was crying. So I watched him drive away and waved. Sighing heavily, I turned with a courageous smile, and entered the dormitory.

As I unpacked my first suitcase, I heard a knock on the door. "Come on in," I called.

"Hi, I'm Linda. I live next door." We chatted for a few minutes and suddenly she asked me, "Are you Mormon?"

My heartbeat raced. "No," I answered, "but no one knows that yet."

"Well," She leaned forward and spoke confidentially, "Neither am I, and I don't intend to become one."

"Hey, all right! Are you a Christian?"

"Yes," she replied. "Of course. Aren't most people?" She

changed the subject. "You know, these Mormons are really strange. Have you heard that they used to practice polygamy?"

I nodded and she continued. "It's true. And they are prejudiced toward Blacks. I want to be friends with Mormons but forget joining their Church."

"Well," I commented, "I'm willing to be everyone's friend, too, but I'm going to be careful about believing these doctrines. I'm glad to meet you. I asked the Lord to bring me some non-Mormon friends."

By late afternoon the dormitory was nearly filled, but I was still waiting to meet my roommate. Finally, I heard a key in the door and a pretty brunette poked her head in.

"Hi, my name's Wendy. You must be my roommate."

"I'm Carol. Welcome! Can I help you move your luggage up?"

We talked as we moved boxes, and I kept wondering how to tell Wendy that I was not LDS. She now knew about my hometown, my family, my academic major, and even my favorite color, but when would I tell her the big secret? I decided to play it safe and keep quiet for a while longer.

At dinnertime several girls from the floor gathered to go down to the cafeteria. Everyone was friendly and excited. I didn't say much—I just listened as the girls talked about their backgrounds, BYU, and the Church. Occasionally I lost the train of thought because they used words I didn't know. Eventually I figured out that the LTM was the Language Training Mission[1] where foreign missionaries spent two months before going to the field. Some girls spoke wistfully of their boyfriends who were at the LTM preparing for missions to places like Peru and Korea. General Authorities, I discovered, are the highest church leaders, such as Apostles, at the headquarters in Salt Lake City. I noticed that the General Authorities commanded high respect from Church members. "Relief Society" sounded like a first-aid organization. I didn't dare ask. Finally, though, I concluded that the Relief Society was the Mormon women's auxiliary—something like a Christian Women's Missionary Union.

I also began to realize that Mormonism was more than a religion—it is a heritage, a culture, and a lifestyle of which each Mormon is proud.

I knew my cover would be blown as soon as anyone asked me anything about the Church, so I decided to break the news to my roommate. Waiting for the right moment that evening, more than once I opened my mouth to speak and shut it again. Finally, I cleared my throat and simply said, "Wendy, I'm not a Mormon."

She stared at me in disbelief. After a moment she said, "Well, what are you?"

"I'm a Christian and a Baptist. I became a Christian last December."

"What are you doing here?"

"BYU is a good school, even for non-Mormons, I hope. I'm here mainly because I feel the Lord brought me."

Wendy was quiet for a while and then she said, "You'll come to church with us this Sunday, won't you? I think you'll like it a lot."

"Maybe. I'll see."

As the word spread among my classmates, I noticed they watched their conversations around me, but they were friendly, even curious, and always willing to include me in their circle of friends. I soon realized that Wendy, and most of my new friends, thought that all non-Mormons were heathens. In fact, they referred to non-LDS as "Gentiles." They thought that anyone who believed in God would surely see the truth of the Mormon Church, and so they assumed I didn't believe anything.

The next morning the freshman students gathered for orientation. Before the session began, one of the students stood and asked whether anyone knew how to lead singing. Several students wanted to form a choir, and they needed a chorister.

I enjoyed conducting music, so I naively volunteered. I didn't realize I was also volunteering to lead the hymn singing that was about to begin. I balked at leading unfamiliar Mormon hymns, but I wasn't going to back out in front of everyone. Not everyone knew I was a Gentile. There were a few hymnals on the chairs, so I grabbed one and hurried to the front.

Because I didn't know which hymns to choose, I asked for requests (an old trick). One student called out, "We Thank Thee, Oh God, for a Prophet" and a moment later, another called out the page number.

"This can't be happening to me," I thought as I cued the pianist. With my head bent over the book, I directed while everyone sang heartily.

When I glanced up, I noticed that I was one of the few using a hymnal. Undaunted, I asked for another favorite. We sang "Praise to the Man Who Communed with Jehovah," another hymn about Joseph Smith. Then, the seminar director stood to make opening remarks. Relieved, I sat down next to Linda.

"Pretty good," she whispered. "No one would have guessed you're a Baptist."

After the announcements, we were dismissed to class. As we began my first class at BYU, the professor asked, "Is anyone here not LDS?"

I winced. I was the only person to raise a hand, and I looked around to see everyone's attention focused on me.

"Welcome to the class," said Brother Greene. (All of our professors were Brothers and Sisters.) I'm sure you will be able to contribute much to our discussions."

Several times during class—a humanities survey—the discussion turned toward religion. Each time it did, I saw my classmates steal a glance at me. Sometimes I was quiet, but sometimes I responded when Brother Greene asked for our opinions. I was struck by how little I knew about Christianity, about the Bible, and about Mormonism.

As the days passed, I began to "fit in" as a non-LDS student at BYU—as a minority. Linda and I were the only Gentiles in the freshman group. I kept most of my opinions to myself, never openly criticizing the Mormon Church, not because I was kind, but because I wanted to hide. I smiled and laughed while on the inside I felt very alone and overwhelmed by the Church's influence.

I learned new things daily about the Church. During dinner one evening, a student asked me, "Why do you wear a cross?"

"Well, I like to." I thought for a moment. "It's a Christian symbol, and it reminds me of the price Christ paid for my salvation." Then it dawned upon me that I had not seen any crosses since arriving in Utah.

The girl responded kindly and patiently. "Latter-day Saints don't believe in the cross. We prefer to emphasize the life rather than the death of the Savior. You don't see crosses on LDS buildings. Worshipping the cross is like idol worship."

I didn't argue—I was speechless. I smiled weakly and looked down at my plate. I had lost my appetite, so I poked at my mashed potatoes for awhile and finally went to my room.

I had worn my cross every day. Now I suddenly realized that by Mormon interpretation, I was an idol worshipper.

Struggling with what to do, I found Paul's words: "For the word of the cross is to those who are perishing foolishness" (I Corinthians 1:18), and "May it never be that I should boast, except in the cross of our Lord Jesus Christ" (Galatians 6:14).

"I am not ashamed of the cross!" I told myself. But should I continue to wear it, knowing how Mormons perceived it, or should I adapt to the culture and put my cross away? The verse about not being a stumbling block came to mind, and I started wearing the symbol of a fish around my neck instead.

Sunday came, and I didn't have a car. The pressure was on, so I decided to get my peers off my back and go to the Mormon Sacrament Meeting. All of BYU was divided into student wards—also known as branches—according to where they lived. I joined the group of students going to the BYU 36th Ward that met in a classroom building.

I dared to sit by Bruce, a handsome student with penetrating blue eyes. I had felt the intensity of his eyes during class, and I wondered what went on behind them. The meeting began with singing and prayer; then the sacrament was passed. I tried to be reverent as first the bread and then the water were passed, but I watched the proceedings curiously. I felt conspicuous as the elements came to me, and I passed them on to the next person without partaking.

After the sacrament, two members of the congregation each gave fifteen minute talks centering on moral and spiritual principles. Then a young looking girl from our group rose to speak. She spoke in a voice so quiet that everyone leaned forward to hear her story. She had been mistreated since childhood and rejected by her parents. Her family never went to church. When she was in high school, a Mormon classmate befriended her and introduced her to the local missionaries. She took the series of lessons they offered, became convinced of the truth of the Church, and wanted to be baptized. Her parents refused to allow it and also rejected the idea of her attending BYU. So she saved her money, waited for her 18th birthday, joined the Church, and was now at BYU for her first semester. Hardly able to choke back the tears, she expressed her love for the Church and her gratitude to the Lord for leading her to the light of the gospel.

By this time people across the room were sniffling and wiping their eyes. Bruce turned to me and said, "She sure has a strong testimony, doesn't she?"

"I guess so," I whispered back. "I'm not a member of the Church."

"Yeah, I wondered about that. I noticed you didn't take the sacrament."

The meeting concluded with another hymn and prayer. The moderator announced that following a short break, a fireside was scheduled for the freshman group.

I asked Bruce, "What's a fireside?"

"We usually have them on Sunday nights," he said. "There's a speaker and someone provides refreshments. It has nothing to do with a fire or anything. By the way, what religion are you?"

"I'm a Christian, a Baptist."

I'd discovered that when I called myself a Christian, Mormons were puzzled. "Well, so am I," they often answered. They needed to place a denominational label on me. I didn't mind. It usually wasn't worth a complicated explanation.

"Oh." After a moment he said, "Tell me, Carol, what do you believe about the Godhead?"

"The Godhead? Is that the same as the Trinity?" I was new at believing—to say nothing of defending—Christian doctrines. "Well," I began, "I believe in God the Father, God the Son, and God the Holy Spirit. Three in one,"

"I'm not talking about the Trinity. We don't believe that. We believe God has a body of flesh and bone, immortal and tangible, and so does His Son, Jesus Christ. The Holy Ghost is the spirit bestowed upon us, but they are three distinct and separate personages, not just different manifestations of the same person."

"Oh." I tried in vain to remember some Scripture verse to support the Trinity. I felt troubled. Fortunately the fireside was about to begin, so we sat down again, our conversation interrupted. The program director asked me if I would once again lead singing.

After the opening prayer, I clutched a hymnal, stepped forward, and announced the hymns (which had, to my relief, been selected in advance). The chairman of an academic department then delivered a captivating talk based on LDS Church principles. However, by now I was tired of listening so intensely and sorting truth from error. I didn't have the mental energy to analyze all I heard.

During his presentation, the speaker mentioned a group of people—called Lamanites—and said, "I'm not critical of them. In fact, maybe some of you are Lamanites." I wondered what a Lamanite might be and even whether I was one.

Later, Bruce escorted me back to the dorm. "Bruce," I asked him, "am I a Lamanite?"

He laughed. "I don't know. Are you?"

"Well, what is a Lamanite?"

Bruce explained, "The *Book of Mormon* contains the record of two ancient peoples who lived on the American continent. The two groups were the Nephites and the Lamanites, and they were always at war with each other. The Lamanites were dark and the Nephites were fair-skinned. In the end, all the Nephites were killed and the Lamanites survived. Their descendants are the tribes of American Indians. So Lamanites are American Indians."

"Well then, I'm not a Lamanite," I concluded. Since I was asking, I had another question. I had read about Zion in the Old Testament, but in Provo I had seen Zion's National Bank, Zion's Park, and Zion's Cooperative Mercantile Institution (a department store known as ZCMI). I wanted to know, "By the way, what is Zion?"

Bruce paused for a moment. "Zion is the city of God. It's where the saints of God dwell. We consider Utah to be Zion because this is where the Latter-Day Saints finally settled."

We reached the dormitory and sat on a bench overlooking the lights of the campus. "Carol, why did you come here?"

I explained, and Bruce said, "So you don't know much about the Church, do you? Would you like to know more?"

"I have no choice, living here. What's on your mind?"

"There are many verses in the Bible that most Christians ignore, but we take seriously—for example, I Corinthians 15:29. Here, read it."

I dutifully read aloud, "Else what shall they do which are baptized for the dead, if the dead rise not at all? why are they then baptized for the dead?" I blinked and silently read it again.

Bruce said, "Did you know that we baptize for the dead?"

"I've never heard of baptism for the dead." I felt ignorant.[2]

"Since baptism is essential to salvation, everyone

deserves the chance to be baptized. So what about all the people who never heard the gospel—the people who lived before the Restoration of the Church? God is loving and fair, and we believe He gives everyone a chance to be saved. Based on I Peter 3:18-20, those people hear the gospel after they die."

Reluctantly I opened the Bible to those verses, wondering what I would find. I read aloud, "For Christ also hath once suffered for sins, the just for the unjust, that he might bring us to God, being put to death in the flesh, but quickened by the Spirit: by which he also went and preached unto the spirits in prison; which sometime were disobedient, when once the longsuffering of God waited in the days of Noah, while the ark was a preparing, wherein few, that is, eight souls were saved by water."

Bruce explained. "So Christ preaches to the people who have died, but they still need to be baptized. We Latter-day Saints have taken the job of tracing our ancestry to find names of those who were not baptized into the Church. Members of the Church today are baptized by proxy in the name of ancestors or other deceased people. It's a big undertaking, but with the help of God, we can eventually baptize everyone who has lived on earth. You see, Carol, God has given us some big tasks to complete in these latter days. But he constantly gives us guidance through His servant, the Prophet. Jesus said, 'Be ye therefore perfect,' and we believe that we can be."

"Well," I said, "I don't believe baptism is essential for salvation."

We sat for a moment in silence and Bruce asked, "Carol, what do you think about the *Book of Mormon*?"

I said, "I haven't read it. But to be honest, I don't believe it is Scripture. In fact," (I used one of the few verses I knew on Bruce) "Revelation 22:18-19 says never to add or take away from the Bible."

"Oh, yes. I know that passage. But we believe it only refers to the book of Revelation. Or it might be a mistranslation. But Carol, even if you can't accept the *Book of Mormon* as Scripture yet, it contains much good counsel. I think you should read it, unless you're afraid to."

"I'm not afraid." But I was tired and wanted to go home. After thanking Bruce for walking me home, I slowly climbed the stairs to my room. I opened the door to see several girls seated on the floor laughing and talking with Wendy. Though I smiled and joined the group, my heart was heavy. I knew I couldn't hold back the tears much longer. I took my Bible and left. Hoping the laundry room would be empty, I hurried down the stairs only to find it locked to prevent students from washing clothes on Sundays. I started outside, but remembered that at midnight the dormitory entrance would be locked. It was already after 11:30. I sank to the cement floor outside the laundry room, put my head on my knees, and began to cry.

"Oh Lord, help. I'm so confused. I've only been here one week, and I'm already so discouraged. I don't even know right from wrong. I don't know truth from error. I don't understand those verses Bruce showed me. Why are they in the Bible anyway? Please, please help me understand. I feel so alone. I need you."

The warmth of the tears on my face was a comfort as I waited silently. I leafed through my Bible and stopped at I Corinthians 10:13. The Holy Spirit spoke to me as I read, "No temptation has overtaken you but such as is common to man; and God is faithful, who will not allow you to be tempted beyond what you are able; but with the temptation will provide the way of escape also, that you may be able to endure it."

The freshman seminar ended. As I moved my belongings to my permanent dormitory, I saw my friend Linda, the other non-LDS honor student.

"Linda," I shouted across the parking lot, "wait a minute!"

She stopped and we walked the remaining distance together. "Well, I see you're moving to Helaman Halls also," she said.

"Yes," I replied, shifting my armful of clothes. "I'm glad we'll be near each other. I'd like to talk with another non-Mormon once in a while."

"Oh, I don't mind talking to Mormons. Have you been to any church meetings yet? I like them a lot," she said.

"I went last Sunday. But I think I'll need to get away from here on Sundays at least."

"Don't you like it here? You're not very open-minded."

I didn't respond right away. Unaware that I would hear that accusation often in the future, I finally said, "No one with firm convictions is completely open-minded."

Later that evening as I was unpacking, Linda came by. "Hey, did you hear there's a testimony meeting tonight? I'm going. Do you want to come?"

"I need to get the room in order before Sharon, my roommate from Phoenix, comes. She'll probably be here tomorrow. I'll pass." I didn't know what a testimony meeting was, but I could guess.

"Okay. Bye." She was gone.

I thought about Linda that evening. She would only be fully accepted by the students if she joined the Mormon Church. To be a Gentile at BYU was to be an outsider. I wondered how long she would last. I wondered how long I would last.[5]

Returning from lunch the next day, I saw my door open. I entered to find a whole family in my room. A father sat on my bed watching a busy woman carrying a small child bustle about. Two young boys brought in a big box, and stopped short when they saw me.

The oldest daughter, about my age, stepped forward. "You must be Carol. I'm Janet Merrill, your roommate. Meet my mother and father. This is Robert and John, my brothers. That's Julie, my little sister."

"Hi," I said weakly, looking around the room. "Are you sure you're my roommate?" As soon as I said it, I knew I was off to a bad start. "What I mean is, I requested someone else for a roommate."

"This is G2204, isn't it? That's where I'm supposed to be. Who were you going to live with?"

"My friend from Phoenix, Sharon Stern." I decided to look into the problem later. Janet was probably as anxious about getting settled as I had been. "Do you need help moving in?" I asked.

"No, all the boxes are up now. Sit down."

Janet's father moved over to make room for me. He cleared his throat, looked at me over the top of his glasses, and asked, "Are you Greek Orthodox?"

I suddenly felt nervous. "Greek Orthodox? No, I'm a Baptist. Greek Orthodox?"

Mrs. Merrill pointed to the poster above my bed, a Christian fish symbol with the Greek word *icthus* written in bold letters. "We knew it was a religious symbol," she explained, "and we guessed that you might be Greek Orthodox." She straightened her posture. "We're all Latter-day Saints."

I discovered later that Sharon had been assigned to another floor by mistake. Since we were all tired of moving and Sharon liked her new roommate, I decided to stay with Janet.

The dormitory orientation meeting was held that evening. As we entered the lobby, we each received a long list of instructions and dormitory regulations. The dorm mother, an intimidating, middle-aged woman, addressed us.

"Girls, please follow along on your regulation sheets while I discuss each item." She explained each rule and the penalty for breaking it. Each student, she pointed out, attended BYU by choice, and by coming had agreed to abide by the school's standards.

"Your rooms will be inspected monthly. Your resident assistant will check your room to make sure it is acceptable.

"Please note the visitation hours. Men are allowed only in the lobby. They are not permitted to enter the residence areas except on alternate Sunday afternoons from 2 to 4 p.m. Your doors are to be left open when men visit your rooms. Any questions?"

After the meeting Janet and I returned to our room. "Well," I asked her, "What do you think of the rules?"

"They're pretty strict. I'm glad though, because rules help us stay on target obeying the commandments of the Lord. They guide us toward godhood. That is the purpose of the Church—to show us the way to obtain exaltation and a place in the Celestial Kingdom."

"What is the Celestial Kingdom?" I asked. "Is that heaven?" I braced myself, knowing I'd asked for another theological discussion.

"Well, we believe there are three levels of heaven: the Celestial, the Terrestial, and the Telestial Kingdoms.

These are degrees of glory that we earn here on earth. Most everyone will go to one of these heavens, except Satan and the sons of perdition. They will go to hell. Most people aren't bad enough to go to hell.

"We who keep all the commandments, receive endowments in the temple, and obtain perfection in this life will go to the Celestial Kingdom where God the Father dwells. We will become gods and goddesses ourselves, and reign over worlds of our own.[3] By that time, though, our Heavenly Father will have progressed to a higher level, so we never actually catch up with Him. This is called eternal progression. You see, we never stop growing, nor does our Heavenly Father, nor His Heavenly Father..."

"Janet, wait," I interrupted. "Who is God's Heavenly Father?"

"Well," she answered, "how do you think our Heavenly Father came into being? Other gods have progressed past our universe, so we have only one God. But God has a God, too."

"But that's polytheism."

"Not really, because *we* only have one God. We only know about the others by revelation to the prophets. If you pray about it, the Lord will show you the truth of these things. Now let me finish telling you about the other two kingdoms. People who live honorable lives but didn't accept the Restored Gospel—the Gentiles—will go to the Terrestrial Kingdom. That's not a bad place, but one cannot be exalted there.

"The Telestial Kingdom is the worst. It's for the wicked of the world, like those who murdered Jesus Christ and Joseph Smith. Did you know the three levels of heaven are taught in the Bible? Here, let me read you I Corinthians 15:40 and 41."

"There are also celestial bodies, and bodies terrestrial:

but the glory of the celestial in one, and the glory of the terrestrial is another. There is one glory of the sun, and another glory of the moon, and another glory of the stars: for one star differeth from another star in glory.' The sun, moon, and stars represent the three levels."

"You have built a whole doctrine of heaven on those verses?" I was amazed.

"No, our other Scriptures fill in the gaps left by the Bible. The *Doctrine and Covenants,* Section 76 gives us more detail about heaven. But I just wanted to show you that even the Bible teaches this."

"What do you believe about the Bible?" I asked her.

"We believe the Bible to be the Word of God as far as it is translated correctly. It has passed through so many hands, especially after the True Apostolic Church was lost from the earth, that we believe it contains many errors in translation. Joseph Smith began writing an inspired version of the Bible, but he was martyred before he finished it. Fortunately, we have modern day Scriptures to complement the Bible.

"By the way, Carol, what do *you* believe about the Bible?" Janet was honestly curious.

I paused, feeling inadequate to express myself. "First, I believe the whole Bible, and I don't believe it has been mistranslated. The Bible, and nothing else, is the basis for our doctrine. It says that we enter God's kingdom by grace and faith, not by our good works. I know that's true, not only because the Bible says so but also because that's what happened to me. I put myself in God's hands by faith, and he began to change me. We believe that each person has direct access to God. We have no church hierarchy as you and the Roman Catholics do."[4]

"Well, Carol, classes start tomorrow. Let's stop talking. I'm tired."

"Yeah, me, too," I answered. "You've challenged my thinking."

We turned out the light and I lay in bed, wondering about my new roommate, a live-in Mormon scholar. I wondered if she would try to convert me. I also wondered if she could succeed.

Notes:

[1] The Language Training Mission has been replaced by the Missionary Training Center, a new complex in Provo, Utah where both foreign and domestic LDS missionaries receive training prior to their missions.

[2] The Apostle Paul, in this famous chapter on the resurrection, cites the pagans of the day, who practiced baptism for the dead, to show that even they believe in life after death. Paul was not advocating the practice.

[3] The teaching that we can become like gods has been around ever since Satan deceived Eve in the Garden of Eden. Many Eastern religions teach their followers to look for "the god within," and New Age philosophy also espouses this doctrine.

[4] I didn't realize it at the time, but Latter-day Saints don't like to be reminded of the similarities between their Church and the Roman Catholic Church—which they call the "Great and Abominable Church."

[5] I rarely saw Linda after that. One day, several months later we met in the lobby and stopped to talk.

"Carol!" she exclaimed. "It's so nice to see you. Everything is going so well for me. Coming to BYU was the best decision I ever made. I met the greatest guy, and we're engaged. Also, I'm going to be baptized this Saturday. Can you come? This is a big moment in my life."

I was sorry to see that Linda, my first non-Mormon friend, had been converted.

Chapter Three

I faced my first day of school with enthusiasm. During the morning, I sat down by a fountain and watched the crowds pass. I marvelled at the beauty of the campus. Every student was neatly dressed and well groomed. The sidewalks were crowded with smiling people. Even strangers greeted each other with a friendly hello and frequently old friends crossed paths—a shout, an embrace, and the pair would step aside to converse for a moment. The traffic, crescendoing to a peak each hour, climaxed with a tardy bell and diminished only to explode again when the class period ended.

The pervasive Mormon influence shook me, though. With few exceptions, every student, teacher, and employee in sight was Mormon. Even the ground I walked on and my dormitory bed were owned by the Latter-day Saints. I was over my head in a sea of Mormonism. I sighed, bowed my head, and turned to my only source of strength. The words of a hymn came into my mind:

I know not why God's wondrous grace
To me He hath made known
Nor why, unworthy, Christ in love
Redeemed me for His own.

But I know whom I have believed,
And am persuaded that He is able
To keep that which I've committed
Unto Him against that day.

I longed for Sunday to come. I had called the Baptist church and the pastor's wife had agreed to pick me up for the service.

On Sunday I arrived at First Baptist Church in time for Sunday School. Some of the students in the college class attended Utah Technical College, a vocational school in Provo, but I was thrilled to meet two BYU students in the class. I wanted to hug them on sight! John Cole and Gary Smith were seasoned BYU veterans. John, a junior, and Gary, a senior, shared a basement apartment. Both had survived a long tenure at BYU, knew more about Momonism than many Mormons, and still hadn't joined the Mormon Church or given up and gone home.

The pastor, Don Plott, came to speak to the college class about establishing a Baptist Student Union at BYU. He explained, "In past years, we've tried to activate student work, but we've only had one or two Christian students. No ongoing ministry has been established, but I believe you can be the start of a real BSU.

"We need to submit names of student officers to the BYU activities office right now, so we can be recognized as an official club. John, will you be the president?"

"Sure, why not?" He seemed willing.

Don Plott continued. "Gary, will you be his vice-president?"

"Glad to."

"Now, Carol," Don spoke to me. "I don't know you well, but can we put your name down as the secretary-treasurer for the BSU?"

"I don't know anything about the BSU. I wouldn't know what to do," I protested.

"That doesn't matter. We just need names right now. There's no one else here to do it."

"Well, okay." I wanted to get involved, but who was I to

lead a Baptist Student Union? I'd been a Baptist for less than a year; I'd never been a secretary, and I'd only learned to write a check two weeks earlier. But why not? Being at BYU was already strange, was it any stranger to be an officer in the new Baptist Student Union?

I found a seat in the small sanctuary as the morning worship was about to begin. There were only about sixty members in the congregation and eight members in the choir, but I was so glad to worship with other believers. It seemed as though years had passed since I'd sung Christian hymns and heard a Bible message. My soul was strengthened by the presence of the Holy Spirit.

"For where two or three have gathered together in My name, there I am in their midst," Jesus said (Matthew 18:20). It was true even in Provo, Utah.

And so the Baptist Student Union at Brigham Young University was begun. Pastor Don Plott, as director of the BSU, opened his home to the students a week later for a cookout and planning meeting. Don, in his late forties, had been converted to Christ as an adult. He loved the Lord and preached the gospel, exposing the errors of Mormon doctrine with zeal. On a page in the back of his Bible I found a collection of verses that contradicted Mormon doctrine.[1]

After dinner, Don stood and called for our attention. "As you know, John Cole has agreed to be our president. This week he will submit our constitution and fill out the application forms so that we'll be a legitimate campus organization. Gary, you, Carol, and Diane, will also have to sign those forms."

"By the way, for the new students, Diane Cross is the only reason we're allowed to have a BSU on campus." I looked at Diane, a slender woman who seemed to be about thirty. I remembered her as the capable pianist I had heard in church. She had a quick, merry laugh.

The pastor continued. "Every campus organization must have a faculty sponsor. Diane teaches piano and because she's willing to sponsor us, we're allowed on campus. Thank you, Diane."

Diane laughed and said, "Thank the Lord."

Don continued. "We'd like to have weekly meetings. Can everyone meet on Monday nights? After we are registered, we'll be able to get together on campus. But for now, it will have to be off campus. Victor, could we have the first meeting at your house?"

Victor Hogstrom was an outstanding student. As a Liberian national, he was one of the few Blacks on campus. Victor was a senior, majoring in Communications and International Relations, and he was well-known on campus. Ironically, he—a Christian—was the producer of a religious news program on the school's widely broadcast television station. Victor interviewed a variety of non-LDS guests on his talk show. He also directed congregational singing at church.

"My place is small," said Victor, "but, yes, we could meet there."

With these plans set, the business meeting broke up, and the guys started tossing a football in the yard. I introduced myself to the one student I hadn't met. I was glad to learn that she lived in my dormitory complex. Dawnena Walkingstick was a Cherokee Indian from North Carolina, new to BYU after two years at another university.

We had been talking a while when I said, "Oh, by the way, did you know you are a Lamanite?"

Dawnena laughed. "That's all they call me here. I'm told I have a special inheritance according to the Book of

Mormon. Also, if I were to join the Church and obey the commandments, they say my skin would gradually turn lighter. White skin is supposed to be a sign of holiness."

We laughed together. It was the start of a long and fast friendship. Dawnena and I would often turn to each other for support when we were discouraged. She helped me keep my perspective. After a traumatic day, she'd say, "Let's go get a Dr. Pepper," and we'd sit and talk out our doubts, or sometimes just speculate about what life would be like at a Christian school in the Bible Belt.

Dawnena and I went to Victor's house on Monday for the first BSU meeting. When we found his basement apartment, we had to agree with him—it *was* small. Floor space was limited to a path alongside the wall. As we sat down on the bed, which practically filled the room, John and Gary arrived. I felt renewed whenever these two warriors were around. They sat crosslegged on the end of the bed and Victor rose from his desk. "Don and Diane called to say they couldn't be here tonight. All the officers are present, though, so we can begin."

John handed me a sheet of paper. "Gary and I went to the Organizations Office and picked up this form. Carol, since you're the secretary-treasurer, you need to fill in the bottom part. We'll do the rest. Oh, listen to this. We're not allowed to schedule our meetings on Monday nights. The secretary said that it's Family Home Evening night and nothing may be scheduled to conflict with it."

"Family Home Evening?" I said. Dawnena and I exchanged puzzled looks. "What's that?"

Gary explained. "Every Monday night, every family meets for a devotional lesson, prayer, an activity, and refreshments. It's not a bad idea."

"But what does that have to do with us?" Dawnena asked. "We're not Mormon, and none of our families are anywhere near here."

"Oh," said John, the veteran, "if you haven't heard about this, you will. Every student branch is divided into 'families.' You are expected to meet with your group, even if you're not LDS. I'd hoped we could substitute Baptist Student Union for Family Home Evening, but we can't. So how about Tuesday nights?"

After some discussion, everyone agreed. John changed the subject. "So what does a BSU do? It seems like we ought to make some plans, but I've never been in a BSU before so I don't know where to begin."

"Neither have I," said Dawnena. Victor, Gary, and I hadn't either.

John made a suggestion. "Don Plott said that a few years ago the students showed a filmstrip series called, 'What Baptists Believe.' He said it was a good way to share the gospel. We could do that sometime."

We sat around, devoid of other ideas, until Victor turned on the television. We watched it together until 11 o'clock. Then John adjourned the meeting, and we planned to meet again the next Tuesday.

The following week, BYU officially recognized our Baptist Student Union. On Tuesday night, we held an official meeting in our official place, a classroom in the business building. Diane Cross, our faculty sponsor, joined us. We sat at the desks and looked at the blackboard.

I asked, "Diane, what is supposed to happen at a BSU meeting?"

She said, "I don't know. Larger BSU's have speakers and fund raising events, but we don't need those right now."

It was a motley crew. The meetings were without agendas or minutes. There were no plans for outreach, evangelism, or discipleship, no sense of purpose and no goals. In spite of this, we craved each other's company. The friendships between us grew strong.

Like the first century Christians, we didn't build a big program, but we met one another's needs. It was a unique Baptist Student Union—but BYU was a unique campus. We didn't need activities. We needed each other. As He always does, God in His own time changed us to be more effective servants for Him. He would have bigger plans for the little BSU at BYU, but He began by building solid-steel bonds of love between us.

And though we loved each other, we struggled to love the Mormons. We coped with the stress of living at BYU by voicing our frustrations. Even though we all had Mormon friends, we often joked about the latest incident from a religion class or the dormitory. We laughed cynically about Deseret Industries (a Mormon-owned manufacturer), Zion's Bank, and Sainthood. Of course, in the company of our Latter-day Saint friends our conversation was kinder, but when we were alone, we were scornful. Sometimes in a moment of repentance, one of us would say, "We shouldn't talk this way about the Mormons," and everyone agreed. But soon we were at it again. We had a lot to learn.

The Baptist Student Union was integrated with the First Baptist Church of Provo, Utah. The church members supported us, the students. They often blessed us with a sack of fresh fruit or an invitation to Sunday dinner. Don Plott devoted a portion of each prayer meeting to the BYU students, and the church offered its limited financial resources to support the BSU activities.

As I lived there, in the heart of Mormon culture, I realized that non-Mormon residents of Provo—just like the non-Mormon students—were minorities. Even today, with all the legislation about discrimination, Gentiles don't find jobs easily in Provo, Utah. Latter-day Saints prefer to hire another Saint rather than give a job to a Gentile. Mormons, understandably, prefer to patronize Mormon-owned businesses as a means of supporting their Church. Although most Utah Saints do not boycott Gentiles, they distrust them and keep their business within the LDS Church.

I discovered that Christian children in Utah understand prejudice. In Mormon towns, Christian school children are ostracized. Some parents refuse to allow their children to play with Gentiles, and teachers may spotlight these students in class. One family told me that their neighbors refused to enter their house because they believed it was demon-possessed. High school students earn credit for LDS religion classes, which are offered on their school grounds during the day. Gentile students in a Mormon high school are outsiders. They aren't members of the local stakes which sponsor youth activities for the students.

First Baptist Church also felt the influence of the Mormons. Often on Sunday mornings two young men, dressed neatly in dark suits, white shirts, and ties, carrying two zippered leatherbound books and a notebook each, entered the service. We knew one book was the King James Bible and the other was the Triple Combination (the *Book of Mormon*, the *Doctrine and Covenants*, and the *Pearl of Great Price*). The visitors were always surprised when we recognized them as Latter-day Saints.

Mormon visitors came to church to observe, but many of them eagerly participated in our Sunday School classes. During the worship services they paid close attention, and most took notes for their own records or because they had come on assignment from a comparative religions class.

As students, we invited our LDS roommates and friends to church. In fact, we sometimes would attend an LDS service with them, and then ask them to visit our church. One night Dawnena brought a dozen friends from her dormitory floor. She introduced them one by one to the congregation. Each squirmed a little as her name was mentioned, and they exchanged glances of apprehension during the service. They were most anxious during the offering—they didn't want to donate money to a false religion, yet felt awkward passing an empty plate. Dawnena assured them that it was fine to drop only the guest card, with their name and address, into the plate as it passed them. We had to admit, it was fun to see our Mormon friends flustered for a change.

One special friend of the church and the Baptist Student Union was my next-door neighbor in the dormitory, a Hong Kong national named Liz Sze. When I discovered that she was not Mormon, I asked her about her religion.

"I'm an atheist," she said flatly.

"Why are you an atheist?" I asked.

"My grandfather was a Baptist preacher in Hong Kong, but I don't need God. It's all foolishness."

Somehow I knew she was holding something back. I talked often with Liz about my experience with Jesus Christ. One day she accepted my invitation to church. "I like to go to church," she replied. Liz's logic baffled me, but she became a regular at church and at the BSU. In fact, she was helpful, dependable, and enthusiastic. She became a good friend to me. But she always claimed to be an atheist.

Once I said to her, "Liz, I don't believe you're an atheist."

Finally the truth came out. "I do believe in God. But I'm not going to be converted. I don't need God. Before I came here all my friends teased me. They said, 'Ha, ha, Liz, you're going to get religious at that Mormon school.' Well, I'm not going to get Mormonism or any other religion."

"That's a bad reason to reject God and live a miserable life."

"I know."

We loved Liz through the whole time we were together. But as far as I know, she never gave her life to Christ.

Note:
[1] See the appendix for this list.

Chapter Four

While the fellowship helped, each of us had to fight some lonely battles. Many of mine came in religion class. Every graduate of BYU is required to complete fourteen semester hours of religion credit. One full year of *Book of Mormon* study is required, but I decided to break in gradually and begin with a New Testament class.

My problems began the first day of class when I could not find the classroom. I stumbled in late and sat in the only empty seat at the center of the front row, practically on top of the professor, Dr. Mackay. He glanced at me as he spoke.

"I assume that you have completed Religion 121-122, *Book of Mormon*. We will refer often to the material from that course. You will rely on your knowledge of the Church as well. Some of you more recent converts to the Church have less background. I understand that, but I expect you to participate intelligently in our class discussions. Class participation will influence your grade.

"Bring your New Testament to class each day. I will be using the Greek testament. By the way, I also teach Greek 101. I earned my Ph.D. in ancient languages."

I was impressed. I was also terrified. What was I, a freshman, a Gentile, doing here? I would have dropped out, but feared that a *Book of Mormon* study might be even scarier. At least I knew something about the New Testament.

My New Testament study began in the Gospel of Matthew. I was in trouble even before we finished Chapter 1. The professor explained the divine conception (the virgin birth of Jesus) by saying that Jesus had received His spiritual life eons before as a result of the union of Heavenly Father and Heavenly Mother. "Before the beginning of time as we know it, all humanity was also spiritually born. We are all spirit children of the Heavenly Father and Heavenly Mother—Jesus is our spiritual brother. Jesus received a body on earth when the Heavenly Father[1] came bodily to earth and had relations with Mary."

I sat speechless at this explanation. Matthew 1:18, the very text we considered, said, "she was found with child of the Holy Ghost." My heart was pounding. I wondered if I should say anything. I was afraid I wouldn't be able to defend myself against a Doctor of Philosophy and a room full of Mormon students.

As I looked around to see how other students reacted to this explanation of the virgin birth, one asked, "What do Protestants believe about the divine conception?"

An amused look spread across Dr. Mackay's face. He said, "The Protestants believe that Jesus was conceived by relations between Joseph the carpenter and Mary."

My eyes widened. I wanted to protest, but I knew I would cry if I tried to speak. I didn't hear a word of the rest of the lecture. After class I summoned my courage, gripped my textbooks, and approached the professor.

"Brother Mackay," I said politely, "I have to question your comment about the Protestants' belief."

"About Jesus' conception?" he said. "Several converts from Protestantism have told me they were taught that

Jesus was born of Joseph and Mary. I can't speak for all Protestants."

I left. I was still too emotional to say much. How I wished I'd had the courage to speak up during class. But deep down I was still afraid of what my classmates would think when they learned I was a Gentile.

Another day we discussed the conflict between Satan and the Church. Dr. Mackay had ccasionally mentioned the "Great and Abominable Church." It made me nervous, and I tried to deduce from the context what he meant. On this day, I was enlightened when a student suggested, "I think there is more to the Abominable Church than just Catholics—anything outside the LDS Church is of the devil."

Several other students murmured agreement. Impulsively, courageously for me, I asked, "Just what is the Great and Abominable Church?"

Dr. Mackay stared hard at the class and said, "Anything, or anyone, not of the Lord, whether or not they are registered on the rolls of the LDS Church." I knew he still thought I was Mormon.

Although our textbook was the New Testament and we also referred to Joseph Smith's "Inspired Version" of the Bible, we actually studied Mormon doctrine. I often caught myself believing what the professor said until he quoted his source: The *Book of Mormon* or the writings of one of the Latter-day Prophets. I was learning to evaluate—not just accept—everything I heard. I kept returning to the Bible as my source for the truth. If I couldn't find it clearly taught in Scripture, I didn't trust it.

But at the same time, I realized that I didn't have to throw knowledge away simply because a Mormon said it. Thinking through Mormon theology forced me to think through my own. If I rejected everything I learned because my professors were Mormon, I'd have to throw away music, history, language, and everything else I was learning. I decided it was much better to be discerning—to filter and evaluate all I heard.

I finally told Dr. Mackay I was a Christian. He was surprised, but I never did tell the whole class. How I wish I'd had the courage to speak up more! When it was over, I received an A in the course. But I wasn't proud of having been silent.

Dormitory life was also a battlefield. There was no escape from the LDS influence. John and Gary had warned us about Family Home Evening. I soon discovered that I was expected to attend. Our branch, or BYU ward, was divided into "families," or activity groups, each with a male and female leader. The peer pressure was strong, and I found myself at my first Family Home Evening meeting.

Janet, my roommate, and I belonged to an activity group with our neighbors, including Liz Sze, and some men from a nearby dormitory. The first meeting was boring. We introduced ourselves, talked about the future meetings, and ate refreshments. From then on, the ladies and men would meet separately—only occasionally did we have joint activities.

The next Monday, the girls met in our room. Janet taught a lesson about love. I spoke up at that Family Home Evening because I felt safer in the small group. Also, I wanted Liz, who was bombarded by Mormons all week, to hear another opinion. Of course, it was easy to talk about love without getting into heavy theology.

Our Family Home Evening became a religious study group. First we studied a doctrinal treatise called *Jesus the*

Christ, by James E. Talmage, one of the twelve LDS apostles. His book was (and is) standard reading in the Church. Another Monday night series was a study of the *Pearl of Great Price*, one of the Latter-day Scriptures. Inevitably, my turn came to lead the discussion. We were in the 5th chapter of Moses, one of the books in the *Pearl of Great Price*. I read aloud:

6. And after many days an angel of the Lord appeared unto Adam, saying: why dost thou offer sacrifices unto the Lord? And Adam said unto him: I know not, save the Lord commanded me.

7. And then the angel spake, saying: This thing is a similitude of the sacrifice of the Only Begotten of the Father, which is full of grace and truth.

8. Wherefore, thou shalt do all that thou doest in the name of the Son, and thou shalt repent and call upon God in the name of the Son forevermore.

This sounded to me like a mixture of the Old and New Testaments. As I finished reading, a voice inside me rose up and said, "How can you sit there and read this, you hypocrite? You're acting like you believe it. You're just trying to fit in with your Mormon friends."

My mind was far from the discussion of the book of Moses as I argued with the voice. "What am I supposed to do? Tell these girls they're following Satan? Or should I just give up here and go back to Arizona?"

"No, just don't be such a chicken. Take a stand for Jesus once in a while."

I returned my attention to the group of girls.

"Look at Moses 5:11," said Cindy, who lived across the hall. We followed as she read.

11. And Eve, his wife, heard all these things and was glad, saying: Were it not for our transgression we never should have had seed, and never should have known good and evil, and the joy of our redemption, and the eternal life which God giveth unto all the obedient.

"Do you see what that says? Because of Adam's transgression, we have the opportunity for eternal life through obedience. So Adam helped us by eating of the fruit."

Everyone agreed, but I said, "Wait a minute. Adam and Eve disobeyed God. How could that be right?"

Janet answered. "Adam was actually obeying the higher, ultimate plan of God. We realize, Carol, that all you believe is the Bible, but the modern Scriptures such as this one give commentary on the Bible. This passage is a perfect example. It fills in the gaps the Bible leaves." She was condescending.

I dropped the matter and let the discussion continue as I talked back to the inner voice. "See? That's what happens. There's no point in these discussions. Someone just puts me down—they don't listen to what I say. They're not going to change. I think I should try to get out of Family Home Evening."

I was learning that discussing doctrine with devout Mormons was not evangelism. Arguing doctrine with Mormons only angered me and strengthened them in their own convictions.[2] Liz had already quit Family Home Evening—she wasn't trying to impress anyone else. I began to ease my way out of the Monday night meetings, but the group was very accommodating and tried to schedule meetings so that I could attend. I finally asked Janet not to expect me any more.

Instead, I decided to look for other non-Mormon students. I asked our resident assistant whether she knew any other non-LDS girls in our dormitory.

She replied, "Have you met Peggy, down at the end of the hall? I think she's some sort of Protestant. And you probably know Tammy, the Lutheran girl."

Both were strangers to me, but I hastened to Peggy's room to introduce myself. A plain, chubby girl answered the door, and I said, "Hi, I'm Carol. Are you Peggy?"

"Yes." She seemed hesitant.

"I live down the hall. I heard that you aren't LDS. I'm not either. I wanted to meet you."

She smiled. "I was baptized last week. Come on in. I'll tell you about it."

As I entered, I saw posters of the Osmond family covering the walls. Peggy motioned to one poster. "I owe a lot to them. It was because of the Osmonds that I found the Church. Back home I listened to all their albums, and one day I read in a magazine that they are Mormons, so I started studying about the Mormon Church and decided to come to BYU. Did you know the Osmonds live right near here? I saw Donny one day.

"Anyway, after coming here I saw the truth of the Church and became a member. You know, before this I was into drugs and everything. The Church has really straightened me out. Carol, if you haven't seen the truth of the Church, you will. I'll pray for you. I'm glad you came down to meet me. Come back anytime."

"Yeah, thanks." Feeling dazed, I started toward Tammy's room, but could not bring myself to visit her. I was too discouraged to risk meeting another Osmond fan. I returned to my room, and found Janet deep in the midst of a conversation with Barbara from our family activity group. Barbara was a recent convert to Mormonism and often questioned the Mormon doctrines she was taught.

"But I can't believe there is a god before our God, and another god before Him, and that we are part of that cycle," Barbara said to Janet.

"Yes, Barbara, these things are hard to understand.

You have to work hard to believe them. When I first heard the story of Noah's Ark, I just laughed. But after a while, I believed it. It takes time and faith."

"But this is different than Noah's Ark." Barbara was perplexed. "That's an event—a flood. I believe God created the world. He could easily cause a flood. But this eternal progression of the gods doesn't make sense at all."

"It will, Barbara, it will. Just be patient." Janet looked up and acknowledged my presence. "Oh, hi, Carol."

"Hi. Sorry to interrupt," I said.

"No problem. We've got to stop talking and start studying," Janet answered. Barbara left, and I sat down and opened my history book.

"Oh, Carol, your visiting teachers came by. I told them to come again later."

I said, "My who?" But I thought, "Now what?"

"Your visiting teachers. The branch has assigned everyone two visiting teachers. They come by once a month to bring a spiritual lesson and to see how you are doing."

"But I'm not in the branch."

"Yes, you are. You're on the rolls. You just aren't active. You also have two home teachers. These men will also come to see you once a month. They are your spiritual guides and can help with whatever you need."

"What happens if I don't want all these teachers?"

"I don't know. Tell them to leave, I guess."

We both sat and tried to study, but Janet felt as restless as I did. She finally laid her books aside and pulled a large scrapbook off the shelf.

"What is that?" I asked.

"This is my Book of Remembrance. Most Saints have one. This first section is my genealogy. The leaders of the

Church counsel us to trace our family history. Because my family has been in the Church for generations, most of our genealogy is done. I just copy and expand it."

"Why do they tell you to do genealogy work?" I asked.

"We are supposed to trace our ancestry back as far as we can—especially to the days before the Restoration of the Church—because those people didn't have the opportunity to hear the gospel and be baptized. So we baptize them by proxy. In fact, next week I am going to the Provo temple to do baptisms."

"Oh, yes. I've heard of baptisms for the dead." I thought of my friend Bruce. "Who do you baptize?"

"Nobody, I am going to *be* baptized as the proxy for people who have died. Church members send in the names of their relatives and as the temple worker baptizes me he says the names of the people. I will probably be baptized about 40 times. Usually young people are the proxies. I've done this before. I always look forward to serving the Lord in this way."

"What else is in that book?" I asked.

"My patriarchal blessing. I can't show it to you because it's very sacred. Do you know what a patriarchal blessing is?"

"No."

"Every Latter-day Saint has the privilege of receiving a blessing from a patriarch, a leader in the Church. I have a record of everything he said in my blessing. The patriarch tells us about our future, about our character, what our special flower is, things like that."

"What is a patriarch?"

"Most every stake has a patriarch. They are the older, distinguished men who have been leaders in the Church."

Living with the Latter-day Saints

"How does the patriarch know what to tell you?"

"It's a revelation from the Lord. The patriarch is very wise and discerns the mind of the Lord. Carol, I wish you could share in all the blessings of the Church. They're so meaningful."

"Janet, I wish you could know Jesus like I do," I said gently.

"Well, I'd better be diligent and study for awhile." Janet stood up and stretched, changing the subject. "I'm starting to get tired."

"Do you know someone on our hall named Tammy?" I wanted to visit the Lutheran girl.

"Oh, yes." Janet smiled. "I see her in Sacrament Meeting every Sunday. She's in room 2210. You should get to know her."

"I'm going to try." Sacrament Meeting every Sunday. This was not good news. I prayed for grace as I trudged down to her room and knocked on the door. I recognized her when she answered,

"Hi, Tammy, I'm Carol."

"Oh, yes, you're the non-LDS from down the hall. I've heard about you. You haven't gotten involved in the branch yet, have you? I'm training to be a visiting teacher right now." Tammy was enthusiastic.

"You're training to be a visiting teacher? Are you a Latter-day Saint?"

"No, but I participate in the branch. Anyone can. Why don't you come?" she asked.

"I'm a Christian, that is, a Baptist. I don't want to participate in the LDS Church."

"Oh, but you're missing out on so much. The whole social life of this school happens in the branches. I met Peter in our branch." Tammy sighed and continued. "We're going to be engaged after I join the Church. Do

Faith Under Fire

you know Peter? His father is one of the General Authorities of the Church. When I turn eighteen and join the Church, his dad is coming down from Salt Lake City to baptize me."

"What do your parents think about it?" I wondered if she were waiting until her eighteenth birthday because of her family.

Tammy looked down. "That's why I have to wait. They are devout Lutherans and would almost rather see me die than join the Mormon Church. I had to save my own money to come here. But I'm glad I did. Anyway, I'll have another family soon."

"I feel sorry for your parents."

She flinched as though I had touched a wound. "Well, I've tried to reason with them, and they just don't understand. They are closed-minded. But I am an individual, and I have to live my own life even if my parents disagree...but I do wish this didn't hurt them so much."

"So do I, for your sake," I was sad. "Tammy, if ever you want to talk with someone outside the Church, come see me."

"Thanks. Thanks for stopping by."

Instead of returning to my room, I went for a walk. The autumn night was fresh and cool, and as I walked, I talked with the Lord.

"Lord, I feel so discouraged. My heart aches for Peggy and Tammy, and for Tammy's family. And for Barbara, who's trying so hard to believe. If only I had found them sooner, maybe they would not have converted. Why didn't I get braver? I've been such a chicken. I'm so sorry.

"The influence here is overwhelming. It seems like every non-Mormon joins the Church. I never know who will be next. What if one of the BSU students becomes a Mormon? I couldn't stand it without Dawnena or John or Gary. Watch over us, please, Lord. Help us to know you better. Please, please don't let us be blinded and join the Mormon Church."

I walked silently and allowed God's comfort to restore my soul. I returned to my room with an aching, but peaceful heart.

In late October Don Plott handed me a computer printout entitled "Baptist by Denomination." He said, "I just received this list from the University. Will you contact these students?"

"Sure." I was getting used to contacting strangers. I looked over the list of about 25 names. "I'm not even on this list. I hardly know any of these people. Where was this list in August when we needed it?"

"Carol, it may not be complete or early, but the school does us a big favor by providing it."

"You're right, Don. Sorry for complaining."

John Cole and I divided the list of students. As I called each person, I prayed that he or she was still "Baptist by Denomination." It was a depressing job. More than half the students said they were now Latter-day Saints or had plans to join the Church. Others weren't interested—they had already established friendships with their LDS classmates and didn't want to be identified with a Baptist group. Not one person I called came to church. It was too late.

I experienced my first General (all Church) Conference in October. This conference, I discovered, was held every October and April and arrests the attention of the LDS world. On Friday and Saturday, selected Apostles and other General Authorities deliver messages. Many classes were dismissed because of the Conference. During the weekend, nearly every television set and radio in Provo was tuned to the messages which were broadcast live over KSL from Salt Lake City. On Saturday as I walked through the dormitory, I heard the speaker's voice droning from each room. Many students who had family or friends in Salt Lake City joined the action at Temple Square and crowded into the Tabernacle where the meetings were held.

I was soon weary of hearing the talks, and I went outside for a walk. Groups of students on the grass were studying while listening to radios. In the student union, the Conference was broadcast over the public address system. I finally found respite in the library.

After President Kimball's closing address on Sunday, the radios were turned off, but a renewed vigor pulsed trough the LDS community. My friends were more zealous than usual in their efforts to convert me.

On Monday night, when Janet returned from Family Home Evening, she said, "Oh, Carol, I invited some people to visit you—the missionaries from our stake. They'll be downstairs in a few minutes."

"You did? You should have asked me first," I protested.

But Janet escorted me to the dormitory lobby where two men stepped forward and shook my hand. "You must be Carol," said one. "I am Elder Brown and this is Elder Pratt. We serve as part-time missionaries in your stake. We're students here, but we have both served two-year missions. We would like to tell you about the series of discussions for investigators of the Church."

I interrupted. "I must tell you that I'm not an investigator. I'm happy in my faith, and frankly, do not plan to join the Church."

"We understand," Elder Brown hastened to assure me. "The purpose of the discussions is simply to teach about the Church. Through these discussions, we will share the history of the Church and its beliefs. We feel it is important for you to keep an open mind and try new ideas before making judgments. We don't want to put pressure on you. We know you are Baptist. These lessons will simply help you understand us better."

"How many discussions do you give?" I asked.

"Seven. When would you like to begin?' asked Elder Pratt.

I felt challenged. I didn't want to appear weak or afraid, but I needed time to think. So I said, "I'd like to wait a couple of weeks."

"Fine. How about starting a week from Sunday at 3:00 p.m.?"

I thought for a moment and awkwardly said, "Well, I guess so."

"Here is my card. Carol, thank you for your time. We look forward to meeting with you." Each elder shook my hand as we parted.

Janet was beaming as we returned to our room. She squeezed my arm and said, "Carol, I'm so happy for you."

"Thanks, Janet." I was anxious, but exhilarated at the thought of taking on the missionaries. I had asked God to make me brave, and here was my chance to show courage.

After a night's sleep, the exhilaration had passed, and I hoped I was as strong and wise as I was brave. I talked to Don Plott about the lessons. He cautioned me against taking them. Dawnena didn't know any more about the lessons than I did.

I mentioned my plan in a letter home, and a few days

later I received a letter back from my father.

Dear Carol,

I am very concerned about your getting involved in the Mormon teaching program. You must be aware that they will do anything they can to win you over. You are a source of great concern to them.

Matthew 7:15 says, "Beware of false prophets, which come to you in sheep's clothing, but inwardly they are ravening wolves." Honey, be very wise; you have accepted a big challenge, and you have a lot at stake. The chance that you will gain any ground in that situation is extremely remote.

Don't feel defeated if the Holy Spirit moves you to back out or bail out in the middle of the program. I feel very strongly that I must alert you to the dangers involved. Sweetheart, we will keep you constantly in our prayers. Let the Lord be your guide.

Love,
Dad

Now my zeal was gone. I decided not to take the lessons. With trepidation, I called Elder Brown.

When he answered, I said, "I am calling to tell you that I have decided against taking the series of discussions at this time."

After a long silence, he said, "Why?"

"Several people, including my father, have counseled against it. I have decided to wait."

"You're afraid, aren't you?" The elder's voice almost dared me.

"No, I am not afraid to take your lessons."

Living with the Latter-day Saints

"Then your father is."

"Elder Brown, don't accuse my parents."

"Carol, I challenge you to discover for yourself the truth of the Church. I promise that you will gain a testimony of the truth of our Church when you take these discussions. What we have to say is very significant and must be considered."

"I'm sorry. I hope you are not offended. My decision is final."

"Have you read the Book of Mormon?" he demanded.

"I have looked it over. I'd rather read the Bible."

"Carol, you know the Bible is incomplete. The Book of Mormon is a supplement to the Bible and fills the gaps it leaves. I challenge you to read it and ask God if these things are true. If you ask with sincere faith and real intent, He will manifest the truth to you."

When I finally hung up the phone, I couldn't hold back the tears.

Janet had heard my side of the conversation and sensed the elder's brusque manner. "Oh that makes me mad," she said. "I'm going to talk with that guy. He had no right to be mean to you."

I laughed in spite of the tears running down my cheeks. "Thanks, Janet. You're so nice to me. I thought I was being too sensitive."

"That elder was being insensitive. I really am going to tell him off. Give me his phone number." Janet, thin-lipped, stomped out of the room to the phone in the lobby.

Soon she returned and said, "Well, I told him. He said he didn't even know he was being rude. He said to tell you he was sorry."

I valued Janet's fierce loyalty to me. She rejected my faith, but she did respect me as her roommate.

The Utah-Idaho Baptist association sponsored a Baptist Student Union fall convention each November. This fall the weekend conference was held in southern Idaho. Diane Cross and Don Plott joined Dawnena, John, Gary, Liz, Victor, and me for the trip to Pocatello. When we arrived, thirty-five students and leaders from other campuses were already present. Murmurs of amazement spread among the students from other schools as they discovered we were from Brigham Young University. After being isolated from the outside world, we were overjoyed to meet Christian peers from other schools.

The BYU delegation had a wonderful weekend. We found answers to the question, "What does a BSU do, anyway?" We found Christians who cared about us. The students from other campuses rallied around us and pledged to pray for us. The BSU and BYU suddenly had an identity. We even volunteered to host the next convention, in spring, at Provo.

At the end of the conference, each campus group told what Christ had done through the BSU on their campus. Don asked Liz to share on behalf of the BYU group. I was eager to hear what she had to say.

Liz walked slowly to the podium and said, "I have seen Christ's love in the BSU at Brigham Young University. I can't understand why they care so much for me. I won't even accept Christ into my life, but they keep on praying for me. . . . I guess that's the love of God. Even though I'm not a Christian, they never give up on me." Liz hesitated, as though deciding whether or not to say more, and walked slowly back to her seat. Don stood to pray for her.

We returned to Provo on Sunday, encouraged by the faith of others and aware that God was working in our lives. The following weeks at school were a race to final exams. It wasn't until Christmas vacation that I had time to reflect on the four months at BYU. God had graciously, richly provided me with friends, a church, and enough faith to face each new challenge. And so far, I was still a Gentile.

Notes:
[1] Joseph Smith taught that God has a body of flesh and bone (*Doctrine & Covenants* 130:22). Brigham Young taught that Adam was God (*Journal of Discourses*, Volume 1, page 50).

[2] See the appendix of this book for help in witnessing to Mormons effectively.

Chapter Five

I returned to Utah on a blustery January evening. The snow, driven by an icy wind, burned my face as I hurried to my dormitory to thaw out.

After unpacking, I dialed Dawnena's number. Her telephone rang unanswered. Gary Smith had graduated in December, but I hoped John would be home. I called him but got no answer there. Feeling anxious, I called Diane Cross. I was relieved when she answered.

"Hi, Carol, welcome back!" she exclaimed. "I've been expecting to hear from you. Victor's back, but I haven't heard from anyone else. We need to plan the BSU activities for this semester. Of course, Gary won't be back, but when John arrives, let's get together to talk about it."

While I talked with Diane, the door opened and Janet staggered in under a load of luggage. I finished my conversation, then greeted her with a hug.

"Hi, roomie, it's good to see you." I said sincerely. I *was* glad to be back. BYU was still strange, but not as frightening as before.

Classes began, but we were still waiting to hear from John and Dawnena. I was perplexed. Finally, during the second week of school, John called me.

"John!" I almost shouted into the telephone. "Where are you?"

"I'm here in Provo, but only for three days. I won't be staying this semester. I can't afford it. I can take every class back home for less than half the cost. I've prayed about this. I just don't have the money for tuition. I came to pack my things."

"But, John," I was panicky, "you're our BSU president!"

"I know. I'm sorry. But don't say good-bye yet. I'll be here until Friday."

Small comfort that was. Friday came and John went home. My dreams for the Baptist Student Union were fading. Gary was gone, and now John was gone. I—the freshman, the young Christian—was now the senior officer.

Victor and I met at Diane's apartment to talk about the future of the BSU. We mostly just stared out the window at the snowy town.

"Well, we are the BSU," I glumly observed.

Victor, with a pompous air, said, "Yes, Miss Carol. You are now the president."

I responded, "I did not volunteer to be president. I was not elected. Can a person become president by default? Victor, I think you should be the president."

"Oh, no. Not me. I'm graduating this spring. My course load is too heavy."

Diane said, "Carol, you'll do fine. I'll work with you. And guess what? Dawnena called. Her grandfather passed away last week. She stayed in North Carolina to help her family."

I asked the question that mattered most. "Is she coming back?"

"She's going to try to make the late registration deadline. That's next Wednesday."

"Let's pray she makes it," I said.

Victor changed the subject. "What is the BSU going to do this winter?"

"Last fall we talked about showing the film series,

'What Baptists Believe.' I still think that's a good idea," offered Diane. "Carol, you haven't seen those. Each filmstrip addresses a different doctrine, such as God, the church, and salvation. We could show a couple each time and have a discussion afterward. For publicity, we can put up posters and advertise in the newspaper. Victor, you work at KBYU-TV. Wouldn't this be a newsworthy item for your show, *Religion Today*?"

"Yes. In fact, since I'm the producer, I'm always looking for guests for our talk show. Guests like you, Carol."

"Oh, no!" I had only been named president a few minutes earlier, and now Victor was asking me to be on television. "Me? Come on!"

Diane quickly echoed his suggestion. "Yes, you. Being on television would be excellent publicity for the BSU."

I thought for a minute and said, "When would it be?

After looking at a calendar, Diane suggested, "The earlier we schedule these films, the better. People get too busy later in the semester. Why not start on January 21st, two weeks from Tuesday? By the way, remember, we volunteered to host the next BSU convention here. It's the weekend of March 28th and 29th. Carol, when you schedule the film series, try to reserve a room in the Wilkinson Center for the convention. We can expect about 30 people."

"In the Wilkinson Center? Do you think they'll let us hold a Baptist convention in the BYU student center?" I asked doubtfully.

"There's no harm in asking."

"Okay. I'll do what I can."

We chuckled at the thought of it. *Maybe this won't be so bad after all*, I thought. Even three of us could make a difference, with God's help. I was a reluctant leader, but so were Moses and Jonah and Gideon. I wasn't the first, nor the last, scaredy-cat in God's service.

The next day I ventured into the scheduling office. The secretary was pleasant, but her greeting became an amazed stare when I asked about scheduling a room for the Baptist film series. However, she put it on the university calendar.

I tried to act casual as I requested a room for the BSU convention in March. This time the secretary stood up and walked into the back office. When she returned, she said, "I just talked with the scheduling director. He approved your request."

We all prayed for Dawnena's return, but still we heard nothing. The evening before registration closed, my telephone rang and a familiar voice said, "Hey, Carol, I made it back in time!"

Victor, Liz, Diane, and I converged in Dawnena's dormitory room. With Dawnena's enthusiasm and support, now I knew I'd make it through the year.

A few days later, while I was at Victor's house, a man from Nigeria stopped by. Victor introduced him as Amos. As he talked with Victor, I noticed Amos's bitter attitude about BYU. When I left, Amos walked with me until we came to his house. I asked him what bothered him about Brigham Young University.

He pierced me with a stare. "Can you imagine how it feels to be hated for the color of your skin? Most people here won't even look me in the eye. I think they're afraid of me. I have been here for two years and not one girl has consented to go anywhere with me. I was friendly to a Mormon girl once, and she returned my kindness with hatred. I vowed never to befriend a Mormon girl again. You are the first non-Mormon girl I have met since then."

I tried to empathize with Amos. "Sometimes I sense prejudice toward me, but not like you do. I'm sorry you have been treated so poorly. You probably think all of America is this way."

"No. I don't see how it could be. I wish I could transfer to another school. Ironically, I'm here on scholarship." We approached a dilapidated house south of the campus. "Here is where I live. I share this house with some other Nigerians. . . .Carol, before you leave, may I ask a favor? I'd like very much to talk with you again. Will you give me your phone number?"

After hearing his story, I could hardly refuse.

I reflected sadly on Amos's plight. Victor wasn't as bitter toward the Mormons, but he had many Christian and Mormon friends. Maybe Amos's experience wasn't typical—and maybe he had lost his perspective.

I decided to ask Janet about the LDS doctrine toward Blacks. I told her about my conversation with Amos and she said, "Well, I think he's exaggerating. The Church is not prejudiced about skin color. But Negroes are descendants of Cain, and anyone with Negro blood carries the curse of Cain. We know from latter-day revelation that Cain's curse was dark skin and Negroid features. Negroes are not equal with other races in regard to certain spiritual blessings. No person of Negro lineage can hold the priesthood or enter the temples.[1] But they can become members of the Church and many have."

"I'm surprised. I wouldn't join a church that believes I'm cursed."

"Carol, the Heavenly Father does love Blacks, but because of the curse, He has placed some limitations on them. We believe that in the future, as man evolves, Blacks will overcome the limitations of the curse and be eligible to hold the priesthood."

That Saturday afternoon Victor called. He said, "I just talked with Amos. He was hurt today, but he wants you to come to dinner at his house. He'll be disappointed if you refuse."

"What happened to him?"

"Come and find out. I told him I would pick you up and bring you over. Can you be ready in half an hour?"

I dreaded what might be ahead. "I'll be ready. Bye."

When Victor and I arrived at Amos's house, two of his roommates stepped out to greet us. "Come in, come in. We've been expecting you."

I wanted to turn and run. The men ushered me into the room where Amos was propped against a pillow, holding an icebag to his face. He adjusted the bag as I entered and I saw his swollen jaw and a black, bruised eye.

Amos motioned me to a chair. I perched nervously on it and said, "Amos, what happened?"

His speech was quiet and labored. "A guy from Tonga came and beat me up. The house next door where he lives has no stove so he came to use ours. He put a pan on the stove and left. I needed to use the burner, so I moved his pot to the back burner. When he walked in the door, he didn't say a word. He just socked my face. That's all I remember until there were policemen in here. Someone took me to the infirmary for X-rays."

"Is anything broken?"

"No, just bruised."

Amos's roommates were standing around. One large, dark man with a deep voice said, "Victor, it's a quarter 'til seven. Are you ready to leave?"

I glanced quickly at Victor, wondering where he was going. I thought he was staying for supper.

Victor saw my glance. "Eddie and I are going to a meeting," he said matter-of-factly. "I'll be back in time to take you home, Carol. Bye."

As they left, I looked around at the four Nigerian men. All were friendly, but I was angry at Victor for leaving me. I turned toward Amos again.

"Tell me about that guy from Tonga. Is he Mormon?"

Amos said, "He's in our branch. I see him there most every Sunday."

"You see him at church? Do you attend the Mormon Church?"

"Yes, why not? We're all members of the Church, except Eddie. He is Seventh-Day Adventist."

"You guys are Mormons?" I was astounded. "Amos, I thought you hated the Mormon Church."

Amos said, "I do. I don't believe any of it. We got baptized into the Church to save the extra tuition money. I don't consider myself a Latter-day Saint. But I did give a talk in church once. I talked about prejudice."

One of the men left to answer a knock on the door. When he returned, two fair-haired young men were with him. An uneasy silence prevailed until one of the guests spoke.

"Amos, we heard about your accident. We're very sorry. We came to see how you are."

Amos, stone-faced, said nothing. The men looked helplessly at me. "We're his home teachers. How is he?"

"I'm all right." Amos interrupted abruptly.

Amos had nothing else to say. Finally, the largest of the Nigerians came downstairs, took the shoulders of both home teachers, and escorted them to the door.

George, another roommate, poked his head in. "Excuse me. Are you ready for dinner?"

Conversation around the table centered on the Latter-day Saints. George said, "The only reason Richard came to see you, Amos, is because he is supposed to. He couldn't care less about you. He's a hypocrite."

To my own surprise, I rose to Richard's defense. "Amos, you didn't give him a chance to care about you. You barely acknowledged his presence."

Amos lashed out—not at me, but at the Mormon culture. "These people, in the name of God, think they are superior to us. Either they ignore us, or they act so condescending it makes me nauseated."

The large man spoke. "I knew it would be like this. I came here to experience hatred."

I fell silent as each man in turn spoke resentfully about the treatment he endured. I knew nothing of the hurt these men expressed. I wanted to believe they were exaggerating, as Janet supposed, but they recounted example after example.

I was relieved when Victor and Eddie returned. I had seen and heard enough for one evening. Victor still had his coat on when I said, "I'd better be going. Victor, can you give me a ride home?"

I gave my regards to Amos and thanked my hosts. Each man shook my hand vigorously and thanked me for coming. I caught another glimpse into their lives when George said, "Thank you for having the courage to come to our house."

After that evening, I went out of my way to be friendly to Amos and other African students. I knew that behind each of those solemn black faces raged a tempest.

We had one week until the "What Baptists Believe" series began. We gathered one evening to make posters and preview the first two filmstrips. I asked Liz to have the posters approved and to post them. Victor told me to report to the KBYU-TV studio on Friday morning at 9:45

Faith Under Fire

for the taping of *Religion Today*.

On Friday morning, looking my best, I reported to the KBYU studio lobby.

"Hello, Miss Avery, please be seated," said the receptionist. "Your interviewer will be out shortly."

Soon a man wearing a classy suit strode into the lobby and glanced around. Since I was the only guest waiting, he said, "Carol Avery, I presume."

He sat down beside me. "I'm David Smith. I will interview you on the air. Tell me about yourself and your work with Baptist Student Union so that I'll know what questions to ask."

I told him all I could about the BSU. Soon Victor appeared in the doorway. "Five minutes, Dave. Oh, hello, Carol. Are you ready for your television debut?"

"Yes, Victor." I wished he weren't so flippant about it. I breathed deeply to quiet my nerves, and I prayed as we entered the set. The heat of the floodlights added to the flush in my cheeks as we sat waiting for our cue.

In spite of my apprehension, I was calm and clearheaded during the interview. Dave asked me about the film series, and about the Baptist Student Union. He stressed the fact that I was a freshman, and that I was the president of the Baptist organization. The five minutes passed quickly, and I was relieved when David closed the interview:

"Thank you, Carol, for being part of our program on *Religion Today*." We sat motionless until the camera shifted to the anchorman. David tiptoed off the set and motioned for me to follow. As I left the studio, he said, "Be sure to watch the show when it's aired tomorrow at 6 p.m."

I was in the dormitory's TV room before 6:00 the next night. Some residents were watching a movie that ended at 6:00 and I asked politely, "Does anyone mind if I watch *Religion Today*?"

They didn't, and I changed the channel in time for my interview. The girls in the room watched the show, looked at me, and looked back to the screen. Finally one said, "That's you, isn't it? You're the president of the Baptist Student Union?"

I nodded. All the girls listened intently to the program. When it ended, one said, "I didn't even know there were Baptists here. I'm surprised they let you have a Baptist Student Union." She looked hard at me.

"Well, we're a campus club like any other, even though we're small. The administration doesn't mind. We don't cause any trouble."

Another girl spoke up. "What *do* Baptists believe, anyway?"

"To begin with, we believe the Bible. Our doctrines come from the Bible. It is our only authority."

The first girl interrupted. "We believe the Bible to be the Word of God as far as it is correctly translated," she parroted from the LDS Articles of Faith.

"Yes, I know," I said. "We also believe that man is by nature sinful and separated from God and can only be saved through faith in Jesus Christ."

She interrupted again. "We believe that man shall become like God by perfect obedience to the commandments."

"Yes, I know." I had learned by now that this type of conversation was fruitless. I calmly added, "I need to leave now, if you'll excuse me. Thank you for allowing me to watch the program."

I knew the girls would continue the discussion without me. They weren't listening to me. They only wanted to tell me "what Mormons believe." I returned to my room to call Liz about the posters for the series.

She said she had posted all of them. The next day I checked some of the bulletin boards she had mentioned. I hunted in several places, but found only one. I was puzzled and that evening I called Liz again.

She said, "I know, Carol. I looked for them today, too. Most are gone. I guess someone took them down."

I was irritated when I told Diane about it. But she wasn't upset. She said, "Maybe they didn't like the thought of a Baptist presentation. Next time we'll use other means of publicity."

We were ready on Tuesday, January 21 for whatever was to come. I arrived early at the Wilkinson Student Center to arrange refreshments and set up the film projector. We had invited Ben Rivera, a deacon from First Baptist Church, to attend and help answer questions.

Just before 7:30, our first guests—two students—arrived. Others followed. When about 15 people were present, we began the film, "What Baptists Believe about God," and then showed "What Baptists Believe about the Bible." Afterwards I, as the moderator, introduced Ben, our expert on Baptist doctrine, and opened the floor for questions. We addressed specific questions about the Trinity and the Mormon Godhead—always a hot spot between Mormons and Christians, but the discussion stayed cordial. When we adjourned, we continued the discussions over cookies and punch.

I asked most of the guests personally what they thought about the presentation. One student said that although he disagreed with our beliefs, he wanted to broaden his knowledge about other religions. Most of the others were curious, friendly, and unthreatened by the presentation.

After most of the students left, I was arranging the chairs and thinking about what a good start we'd had—

friendly discussions, warm feelings. Maybe some seeds had been planted. I hoped some of the same people would return next week.

Suddenly I heard a loud voice behind me say, "No! That's not right. You're twisting that verse!" I turned to see a middle-aged man who had watched the films shouting and waving his Bible in Ben's face. I stood back and listened.

Ben responded in a level voice, "It says, 'No man hath seen God at any time.'[2] There's nothing to twist."

"Then it's a mistranslation," the angry man spoke again. "It can't be true because man *has* seen God. He came to earth and appeared bodily to Joseph Smith."

"The Bible teaches that God is a Spirit," Ben said. "For instance, John 4:24."

The man snapped three pages over in his Bible and read the reference, "God is a Spirit: and they that worship him must worship him in spirit and in truth" (KJV).

He slammed the book shut and said, "There's no point in carrying this any further. We have different opinions and can't seem to work them out."

He reached for his coat, and as he left Ben said, "I will pray for you."

The man turned quickly and glared at him. "You don't need to do that."

"I know," replied Ben, "but I would like to."

"I prefer that you don't. The truth I have is so superior to your prayers that your prayers won't matter anyway. So please don't pray for me."

He swept out of the room, and when the door closed behind him, Diane, Ben, and I exchanged glances of relief. Diane had also overheard the conversation.

"What was his problem?" Diane wondered aloud. "You'd think he was afraid of your prayers."

"I am going to pray for him," said Ben. "And I'm going to pray that I'll handle any other confrontations with restraint. When talking with someone like him, it's easy to descend to his level. I wonder if he'll be back."

The audience was smaller for the next three Tuesdays. Most were newcomers—only two or three returned from the first session. The middle-aged man stayed home. There was no more shouting. At the final meeting, Ben, who was a member of Gideons International, brought Bibles to distribute. The Mormon guests, most of whom already owned Bibles, accepted our gesture politely.

After our last film, we evaluated the project. We hadn't seen anyone come to Christ. But dozens, maybe even hundreds, had heard about the Baptist Student Union. We had appeared in the newspaper and on television, but it was not harvest time at BYU. We were still planting seeds.

I thought, "We *can* make a difference here. Before long, Brigham Young University will know that there are Christians on this campus." I felt confident, ready to tackle new challenges. Then I realized who had benefited most from the film series. It was me, the BSU president.

Notes:

[1] The "Negro question" was resolved on June 9, 1978.

"In perhaps the most historic announcement in Church history since 1890 when the Manifesto was issued ending polygamy, the First Presidency announced the revelation that worthy men of all races would be eligible to receive the priesthood." (*1987 Church Almanac*, Salt Lake City: Deseret News, 1986, p.103)

[2] John 1:18 (KJV).

Chapter Six

"Rrrring!"

I awoke to the rude sound of my alarm clock, slapped it, and stared it in the face. It was 3:30 in the morning. My groggy memory focused when I saw my French horn and suitcase on the floor. The BYU Wind Ensemble tour was to begin that morning with bus check at 4:30. I staggered out of bed, stumbled down to the bathroom, and splashed my face with cold water.

When I returned to my room, the light was on, Janet was out of bed, and a continental breakfast sat on my desk.

"Good morning!" she said cheerfully. "I didn't want you to be hungry this morning."

"Janet! Thank you!"

"I arranged for the girl downstairs to walk with you to the bus because the sun won't be up yet. She'll be here at 4:15."

"You're so nice to me," I exclaimed. I hugged her and said, "Now you can go back to sleep. I'll see you next Saturday."

The Wind Ensemble had a long ride ahead that day. The climax of our tour was a concert for the College Band Directors' National Association at the University of California at Berkeley. Each night along the way we stayed in homes of LDS Church members. Our first stop was Reno, Nevada, for a concert at the local LDS stake center.

We began every bus ride and every concert with prayer. After we warmed up and tuned our instruments, we gathered for a devotional before walking on stage. During that week, my respect for the Latter-day Saints' sincere devotion to their Church grew. Every home I stayed in was a model of kindness and hospitality. These Mormons loved each other, and they loved their church.

Since I was the only Gentile in the band, on long, tiresome bus rides my peers were eager to engage me in religious discussions. I resolved not to become angry even when I lost an argument with a veteran Mormon missionary. I still couldn't find everything in the Bible. But pointed questions, intended to make me doubt, drove me to again prove Christianity to myself.

On Saturday night, a host family brought us home for dinner. During the meal Mr. Pratt, our host, said, "Eat heartily—tomorrow is Fast Sunday. Our Fast and Testimony Meeting lasts until 6:30 p.m., so we won't eat again until tomorrow night."

Later on, Mrs. Pratt, my hostess, asked me about my own custom for Fast Sunday; she wondered whether I was accustomed to a light snack or drink in the morning. Politely I answered, "I'm not a Latter-day Saint, but I will join with you in your custom."

"Oh!" A horrified look, quickly masked by a smile, flashed across the woman's face. "I'm so sorry. I will fix you a meal tomorrow." I'm sure she hadn't expected to house a Gentile from Brigham Young University.

"Thank you, but please don't. I'd prefer to fast with you tomorrow."

Mrs. Pratt hardly spoke with me after that. She never got over the shock. Her husband, however, became an aggressive proselytor. I endured patiently the same discussions I had endured many, many times before. I knew enough by now to take either side in the debate.

We spent Sunday in multiple Church meetings. During morning Sunday School we sang a familiar evangelical tune—which I knew as "I Will Sing of My Redeemer"—with unfamiliar words. I choked over the words as I read the theology:

Oh, My Father

1. Oh, my Father, Thou that dwellest in the high and glorious place,
When shall I regain Thy presence and again behold Thy face?
In Thy holy habitation, did my spirit once reside?
In my first primeval childhood, was I nurtured near Thy side? (emphasis mine)
2. For a wise and glorious purpose Thou hast placed me here on earth,
And withheld the recollection of my former friends and birth.
Yet oft times a secret something whispered, "You're a stranger here,"
And I felt that I had wandered from a more exalted sphere. (emphasis mine)
3. I had learned to call Thee Father through Thy spirit from on high,
But until the key of knowledge was restored I knew not why.
In the heavens are parents single? No, the thought makes reason stare!
Truth is reason, truth eternal tells me I've a mother there. (emphasis mine)

4. When I leave this frail existence, when I lay this mortal by,
Father, Mother, may I meet you in your royal courts on high? (emphasis mine)
Then at length when I've completed all you sent me forth to do,
With your mutual approbation let me come and dwell with you.

During that afternoon Mr. Pratt suggested that in order to forget our hunger, we leave the house and visit the Oakland Temple. He had gone several times and participated in the secret ceremonies inside, but wanted me to see the temple and the visitors center.

We returned to the ward in time for the Fast and Testimony Meeting. We sang more songs, received the sacrament, and several people gave testimonies. Mine was not the only stomach rumbling, and I was not the only person glancing frequently at my watch. The family I was staying with finally went home to dinner, and afterward we were whisked off to a fireside given in honor of the band. By bedtime, I would have cried at the mention of one more Mormon meeting.

But by morning I was ready to be strong again. I spent precious time with God on the bus as we drove to Berkeley. Today's concert was the culmination of our tour. Brother Dayly, our director, led the devotional before the concert.

"I would like to share my testimony with you. I know that God lives and has a body of flesh and bone, and I know that Jesus is the Christ. I know that Jesus Christ and our Heavenly Father appeared to Joseph Smith and that this is the Restored Church on the earth today. I testify and believe with every bone and fiber of my body and soul that this is the True Church. I say these things in the name of Jesus Christ. Amen."

"Amen," echoed everyone else solemnly. As Brother Dayly shared, I could sense the strengthening occurring in each person's faith. Everyone's except mine. I had grown to love these people. How could they all be dead wrong?

That week I learned an important lesson. God loves Mormon people...just as He loves everyone who does not know Him personally. Supernatural, unconditional love flowed through me to my Mormon friends, and I knew it was God Himself loving them through me. Ever since I'd come to BYU, I had been so busy defending myself against the Mormons that I hadn't loved them. But a week in isolation with Saints who cared about me had softened my heart.

I also discovered that love opens many doors. I found a new freedom to talk with Janet because no matter what she said or thought about me, I loved her.

Janet was a member of the BYU Latin American Folk Dancers. Usually the group performed off campus, but one Saturday she said, "Why don't you come and see us dance today? We're performing for the Spanish speaking missionaries at the Language Training Missions."[1]

"But Janet, I'm not allowed to go there." I had heard of the strict regulations at the LTM—that section of campus was mysteriously off-limits.

"I'm sure you can attend a program there. Let's see...you've got to dress like a missionary so you won't be out of place. Wear a conservative-looking dress."

Although my dresses conformed to the BYU dress code, none had the "sister missionary" look. "Nothing seems to be right," I concluded after staring into my closet.

"Well, let's see what I have." Janet and I wore the same size. After rummaging through her wardrobe Janet brought out a skirt and jacket. "Try this on," she said.

It fit. I made my face look somber and said, "Do I look okay?"

"Yes, you look marvelous. The program starts at 4:00. I need to go early. I'll just see you there."

I arrived just before four o'clock at the clandestine complex that comprised the Language Training Mission. I had no idea where to find Janet, but eventually found the auditorium.

I sat down near the exit. Soon the dancers entered in bright native costumes. I was relieved to see Janet among them as the show began. I enjoyed the program, but was more interested in observing the audience. When the program ended and the last applause died down, solemnity once again prevailed. Only a few hushed voices could be heard as the missionaries filed out. I tried to look solemn as I slipped out the door.

"How did you like the program?" Janet asked me that evening in the dining hall.

"I liked it very much. And more than anything, I enjoyed seeing the Language Training Mission."

"Yes," Janet agreed. "It was such a privilege for me to serve the Church by performing for the missionaries. And to see all of those handsome men! They will make good husbands in a couple of years." Janet had been corresponding with a young man from her hometown who was now a missionary in Germany.

"I've noticed that many girls here are waiting for a missionary to return or else they're looking around to find one who has just returned. Everyone wants to get married early."

"Yes, we call it the M.R.S. degree," Janet laughed. *"I'm

also here to get an education. But marriage is important. The Church counsels us to marry. You see, part of our responsibility as humans who have been born into bodies is to pass the opportunity to other spirits now in the premortal existence. Unless they are born into the world, those spirits cannot obtain Godhood. Marriage is also important because it is part of our salvation. The Church leaders have told us that we cannot enter the Celestial Kingdom unless we have been married in the temple. In fact, our husbands will raise us at the resurrection."

"Most girls would rather marry returned missionaries, right?"

"Of course. Men are supposed to serve missions, and if they don't, then they aren't totally obedient to the Church. Some men, of course, are physically handicapped and can't serve a mission. But I expect to marry a returned missionary."

We had both finished our meal. After we placed our trays on the conveyor belt, we walked toward the door. "Hey, let's check the mail," Janet suggested.

We stopped at our box, peeked inside, and saw a package slip to redeem at the desk. We waited expectantly while the clerk retrieved the package.

"Oh, Carol, it's for you," said Janet. I opened the small brown package to find a New American Standard New Testament from my older brother.

Just then, Joseph, a friend of Janet's, approached us. "Hi, Janet. Hi, Carol. Hey, you got a package. What is it?"

"It's a Bible from my brother." I smiled hesitantly as I showed it to Joseph.

"Let's see it." He glanced at the cover and leafed through the first pages. "This isn't the King James Version. Carol, I know you aren't LDS, but didn't you know that the King James is the most accurate?"

I replied, "I don't agree. The language, although it is poetic, has changed in meaning since 1611. We don't have to throw it out, but some other translations are more readable and just as acceptable."

"Well!" Joseph exclaimed. "You shouldn't use any other translation. I hope our Heavenly Father has mercy on you."

Janet and I returned quietly to our dormitory room. I felt hurt by Joseph's attack and did not expect any sympathy from Janet. Finally I said, "Joseph's words made me wince."

"I'm sorry, Carol, but I hope you pay attention to what he said. He spoke the truth."

"I knew you would agree with him."

But from then on, when talking with Mormons, I used only the King James Version. It wasn't worth fighting over which translation to use. There were more important issues to discuss.

In spite of my studies, music practice, and daily confrontations with Mormonism, I hadn't forgotten about the Baptist Student Union convention. I confirmed our reservations in the Wilkinson Student Center and arranged for BYU Food Services to cater a banquet for the opening meeting. Baptist students from across Utah and Idaho were attending, and members of the church had volunteered to host students in their homes. The state Baptist student ministries director planned the program, invited speakers, and scheduled time for a tour of the BYU campus.

The day everyone arrived, the BYU daily newspaper ran a story on the convention. According to the article, ours was the first non-LDS religious convention ever held at BYU. Reporters interviewed Don Plott, who reassured them that the Baptists were not coming to proselytize, only to hold meetings. Ironically, printed alongside the article was a notice about a lecture to be given by Hugh Nibley, one of the foremost Latter-day Saint scholars, on the same evening in the room next door to ours.

Before dinner, carloads of students and BSU directors began to arrive. The BYU students were present to welcome them; we recognized many faces from the fall convention. Those who had never visited our campus were awed by its beauty.

One student observed, "Everything is so Mormon! From the statue of Brigham Young to quotations of prophets inscribed on the walls, you're surrounded. I almost feel like a Mormon just being here."

The banquet was superb, the meetings were a success, and we had enough homes to host all the students. On Saturday afternoon we led a tour around the campus, pointing out landmarks and interspersing our comments with episodes about life at Brigham Young University. The visitors were appropriately impressed with the beauty of the campus and the stories we told. Everyone returned home with a new understanding of Mormonism.

Soon after the convention, finals brought the semester to a close. My first year at Brigham Young was over. I went home to Arizona to find a summer job and to gather strength to tackle my second year as a Baptist at Brigham Young University.

Notes:
[1] Missionaries no longer receive training at the Language Training Mission. All LDS missionaries are now trained at the recently built Missionary Training Center in Provo, Utah.

Chapter Seven

Summer was over. I settled back in my seat, preparing for the long bus ride from Phoenix to Provo. I was rested and ready for another year at BYU. Two weeks earlier Diane Cross had called me from Provo with a new adventure.

"Carol," she had said, "you'll never believe this. The BYU Centennial Committee invited the Baptist Student Union to enter a float in the Homecoming Parade. They're putting on a big show this year because of the University's centennial celebration. The church voted to help pay for the float—*our* float! We need to choose a theme that relates to the history of BYU or of the United States. Think and pray about it, then tell me your ideas."

During those two weeks I prayed that God would give us a good theme for the float. As I lay in bed the night I got the phone call from Diane, I kept thinking about religious freedom, an important aspect of American History.

That Sunday, I spoke with my pastor at North Phoenix Baptist Church; I told him we'd be building a float for the BYU parade. Before I could mention that we needed a theme, he said, "You ought to do it on religious freedom in America. You know, Roger Williams, the man who fought for religious freedom, was a Baptist."

"That's a great idea!" I said, and decided to take it back as a suggestion for Diane.

Living with the Latter-day Saints

As I stared out the window of the bus, I thought about the year ahead. I was moving out of the dormitory into Heritage Halls, a complex of university-owned apartments for women. Six women occupied each three bedroom suite. Janet and I had arranged with four women from the dormitory—all Latter-day Saints—to share the apartment. One of them was Sharon Stern, my horn player friend from Arizona.

I'd learned that my time was better spent looking for Gentiles at BYU than trying to evangelize Mormons. Because religion was so important at BYU, students who had never considered God were forced to form an opinion about Him. So I purposed to find non-Latter-day Saints who might be open to the gospel, feeling that, at least, they wouldn't try to argue with me all the time.

The bus finally rolled into Provo. I called Diane who came to meet me. She was preparing lunch for Dawnena, who was back in town early, too. So I joined them.

Over lunch we talked about our goals for the year. "Let's meet during the day every week, so more people can come," Diane said. "All we need is a room to eat lunch in and spend an hour together in Bible study and fellowship."

"That sounds like a good idea. What about Tuesdays at noon?" Dawnena was the vice-president of the BSU for the next year.

I added, "We'll need publicity right away; we need to meet new non-Mormons before they join the Church."

Dawnena said, "Our posters didn't work very well last year. Remember how they disappeared?"

I said, "What about calling the non-Mormon churches in town and asking them to announce our meetings in their churches?"

Diane replied, "That would help. And we do have some

money in our account. We could purchase an advertisement in the school paper. Dawnena, you're in communications. Will you take care of that?"

"Sure," she agreed. "I'll try to design the ad, too."

The next day I visited the Organizations Office, knowing we had to re-register our club before we could schedule any rooms. I completed several forms, obtained signatures, and answered questions. The Baptist Student Union was back in business.

On Tuesday at noon we held our first meeting. As we opened our lunch bags, three new students entered the room. We listened with interest while they introduced themselves.

"My name is Cindy. I'm a freshman. I noticed in the paper that your meeting is open to everyone. I'm LDS. But, you see, my boyfriend back home is Baptist. We made a deal that he would learn about Mormonism if I would learn about his religion. So I'm here."

The next visitor spoke. "My name is Joel Miller. I came to BYU on a tennis scholarship. This morning a copy of the paper was lying open on the tennis court. I couldn't believe my eyes when I saw that ad for Baptist students. I'm not a Baptist, but I accepted Christ a few months ago. So far, you're the first Christians I've met. I was getting discouraged because everyone else around here is Mormon."

Dawnena nodded and said, "We know the feeling."

After a pause, the third visitor introduced himself. "I was at the First Baptist Church on Sunday, and I heard about this lunch meeting. My name is Bob Clark. I'm from Indiana, and I'm here to work on my Master's degree in business administration. I was hoping to get to know some non-Mormons."

Living with the Latter-day Saints

We were off to a good start. The BSU was already growing.

I decided to look for non-Mormons in the dormitories. I went to the residence hall office and asked the receptionist if she had a list of Baptist student residents.

"We don't," she said, "but you're welcome to look through the resident information cards." She motioned toward two file drawers of three-by-five cards. I was surprised that she offered me access to it. I was also overwhelmed at the thought of reading hundreds of cards, but I thanked her and approached the project willingly.

After "religious preference," almost every card said "LDS." I did find a few marked with a Catholic or Protestant preference and noted their names and room numbers.

An hour later, the task completed, I gathered my courage and punched the elevator button. Emerging on the sixth floor, I wandered down the hallway until I found the first room on my list. I knocked on the door, but no one answered.

The next room on my list, one floor up, belonged to a girl who had marked "Christian" as her religion. I knocked on the door, introduced myself, and asked for Susan.

She smiled and said, "I'm Susan. Come in. This is my roommate, Becky. Becky, this is Carol from the Baptist Student Union."

"Oh, hi." From Becky's startled look, I guessed that she was LDS. I soon realized that I had walked into the midst of an involved discussion about the good-looking men in the other dormitory, and my presence went unnoticed. After a few minutes, I wrote my name and number on a card, gave it to Susan, and slipped away.

My next stop was Helaman Halls. I knocked on the first door and a pretty, red-haired girl answered. When I introduced myself, she said, "You're from the Baptist Student Union? Really? I'm Jane, from Waco, Texas. We have a big Baptist Student Union out there. I'm so glad to meet you. I heard there's another Baptist downstairs, but so far I haven't had the nerve to try to find her."

"Why don't we go and look for her together?" I was delighted at the thought of having someone else to visit with me. We stopped at the front desk, and I asked the clerk if she knew of a Baptist girl on the first floor.

She looked at us curiously and said, "Oh, are you Baptists? I heard there's a Baptist club on campus. I think I know the girl you're talking about. Yes, here's her card. Nancy Barnes, in room 1107. She's the only non-LDS girl I know about besides Jane."

"Thanks very much for your help." We walked down to room 1107 and found the door ajar. I looked in and saw a girl studying at the desk.

"Nancy?" I said.

The girl looked up and said, "Nancy's down the hall washing her hair. She'll be back in just a minute. Have a seat."

Before long, Nancy entered with a towel wrapped around her head. She stopped when she saw us and looked at her roommate, who was studying, ignoring us. "Are you here to see me?" Nancy asked. "I don't know you, do I?"

"Hi, Nancy, I'm Carol Avery from the Baptist Student Union. I came to tell you about our club."

"Well, praise the Lord. I've been wondering how to get in touch with some Christians."

We talked happily for several minutes. Jane decided to walk to the dining hall with Nancy. As I left, I invited both girls to church on Sunday and to a picnic afterward.

The next week, Diane brought them to Sunday School. When the class gathered, I noticed a new person who had entered alone. She said, "My name is Cindy Brodie. I'm from Fort Worth, Texas. I really wanted to come to a Baptist church this morning, so I called a taxi."

Bob Clark and Joel Miller, whom we had met at the Tuesday meeting, both appeared for Sunday School. The group was vibrant and excited. With all the new people present, I was uncomfortably aware of how often and how critically we spoke about the Mormons, but I didn't say anything.

We separated after church and hurried home to get dressed for lunch at Sundance, a nearby ski resort, which in early September made a perfect picnic ground. After spending several hours in the warm sun, roasting hot dogs, tossing frisbees, and talking, everyone felt at ease, and I rejoiced to see new friendships developing.

We came down the mountain in time to attend a gathering for non-Mormons sponsored by the Catholic church. While circulating among the group of fifty students, I was surprised to see the graduate assistant from my music class.

"Larry," I exclaimed, "I didn't expect to see you here."

He said," I didn't know you weren't LDS. Your name is Carol, isn't it?"

"Yes. I'm involved with the Baptist Student Union."

I invited Larry to have lunch with the BSU on Tuesday. He came, and later attended other activities. He felt at home with the Baptist students, and I often talked with him in music theory class.

One evening we went to dinner and Larry said, "I've been spending time with all of you recently. I've noticed something different about you—some kind of sparkle. It almost bothers me, but I like it."

"Larry," I said, "what's different about us is our relationship with God. Each of us has asked Jesus Christ to be our personal Savior. He actually lives in us. He's the sparkle you see. It happens by faith, and all we do is accept His salvation as a gift. You can't earn *that* kind of relationship with God."

"Believe me, I know. I'd never deserve it."

"You can accept Christ into your life right now if you choose to. Let me show you a little booklet that explains what I'm talking about." I had a copy of the "Four Spiritual Laws" in my purse.

He read through it with interest, and then said, "Yes. This is exactly what I need to do. I can hardly believe I've come this far in life, going to church and everything, and I hadn't figured this out."

"Would you like to pray right now?"

"Right here? No, not really. But may I take this booklet? I'd like to take care of this tonight."

The next morning I saw Larry. He was sparkling.

I casually said, "How are you?"

"Great!" he answered. "I feel like a new man."

"You are."

I gave Larry some Bible study materials and shared with him from the Bible whenever I could. He eagerly soaked up spiritual truth. However, his two roommates, both returned missionaries, constantly pressured him to become a Mormon. Eventually he quit attending church and BSU activities because he was tired of hassling with them about it.

One day Larry called me. He sounded very discouraged. "Carol, I hope you wouldn't mind if I joined the Mormon Church."

I was silent for a moment. I finally said, "Why would you join the Church?"

"I think that life would be less trouble if I were Mormon. Everything here is based around the Church, and I'm tired of fighting it."

We talked for awhile, but I couldn't talk Larry out of his confused state of mind. I couldn't force him to come to church or to read the Bible. I realized that all I could do was pray for him.

A month later when I talked again with Larry about his spiritual life, his attitude was better. "This is my last semester here," he said. "I decided to go somewhere else for this degree. I realized I could never become a Mormon."

"Oh, really?" I said. "How did you realize that?"

"I can't say exactly," he answered, "but something inside me just told me."

We hadn't yet designed our float for the homecoming parade, and October 11th was only weeks away. Diane and I finally met to plan. To depict our theme of religious freedom, we decided to build an old-time country church structure and have several of us dressed as pioneers attending "Sunday meeting." We rented a float bed from a supplier, so all we had to do was build the superstructure of a church altar and small pews. A skilled carpenter in the church and several other members helped us construct the float. My Mormon roommates helped me build a stained glass window for the front of the church.

The manager of the local Lincoln Mercury dealership agreed to loan us a courtesy Continental to tow the float. Guy Ward, director of Baptist student ministries in Utah and Idaho, came down from Salt Lake City to drive it.

The result was a very handsome church with a stained glass window, three rows of miniature pews, and a pulpit boasting a large white cross. On the morning of the parade, each float was towed to the starting point.

As we towed ours out of the warehouse, we were dismayed to see that the church structure appeared to be too tall to clear the warehouse doorway. Diane prayed frantically for God to protect it. The top cleared the doorway by a fraction of an inch.

At 7:00 a.m. we all gathered at the starting grounds, dressed in our pioneer finery. As we waited for the parade to begin, we wandered the parking lot admiring the other floats. We noticed with surprise that ours was the only float with a religious theme.

Finally, the parade began. As we rode down University Avenue we played a tape of gospel hymns and sang along heartily. The streets were packed with spectators, many of whom applauded as we passed by. Near the end of the route, as we were in front of the dignitaries' grandstand, the parade paused to take up slack. I heard applause again and turned to see Dallin Oaks, the president of BYU, and Spencer W. Kimball, the prophet of the Mormon Church, smiling and waving. We returned the wave, and my heartbeat quickened as we continued to sing our testimony in music.

I didn't return to the warehouse after the parade, but Diane did. The next day she told me, "Carol, do you remember that close call with the doorway at the warehouse? Yesterday afternoon, when we were returning the float to be dismantled, we drove through that same doorway. This time is didn't clear. The doorway smashed off the top of the church."

I was amazed. "Sounds like a miracle to me," I said.[1]

That semester God began to do some refining work in my heart and attitudes. He had taught me to love Janet and my other Mormon roommates and classmates. But still I joined in with my Baptist friends in joking about the Mormon Church. The new students provided plenty of source material for humor as they experienced quirks of Mormon doctrine and practice for the first time. We, who were now the veterans, laughed with sympathy and retold the stories of our first experiences at BYU.

I laughed as hard as anyone, but my spirit was troubled. I was forced to deal with the problem when Bob Clark, one of the new students, took me aside. He said, "I've been to the BSU several times. The first time I came, I almost decided not to return. I was shocked by your comments about Mormons. You are more prejudiced than they are. I only came back because I had nowhere else to go."

I felt defensive. "Bob, we're not prejudiced against the Mormons. I really do love and accept them."

"It doesn't show in your talk."

His words burned in my mind, and I asked the Lord for wisdom. I realized that our critical spirit was rooted in fear. We were afraid that if we were too accepting of Mormons, they would overwhelm us, so we kept them at a distance. We could not accept Mormon doctrine because it conflicted with the Bible, but Jesus called us to love Mormon people.

While I was contemplating these ideas, Diane, who had heard Bob's comments, also asked God for conviction and wisdom. I was glad when, a few days later, she told me, "Our attitude is hindering the Lord's work. I think the jokes about Zion, the temple garments Mormons wear,[2] and being "gods in embryo" are inappropriate. We can learn to evaluate Mormon doctrine in a more Christian manner."

I humbly said, "I agree. Let's ask God to renew our minds—and will you remind me if you hear me say something cynical?"

Diane and I voiced our concern, and the renewal spread among the non-Mormon students. Occasional negative comments were met by at least one stern, loving glare. The result was freedom from thoughts that we never knew had bound us.

I also discovered that often, when God teaches us a lesson, He gives us opportunities to apply it in our lives. My roommates provided me with just this opportunity. The girls were good friends, but sometimes the combined influence of five amateur missionaries wore me down.

We all ate dinner together. One night, someone suggested that we also have "family prayer" together each day. Everyone thought it was a wonderful idea, except me. I felt uneasy and dishonest when I prayed with Mormons, because praying to their concept of God—an exalted man—was praying to a false god. In fact, it felt like blasphemy.

During the conversation, I kept quiet, hoping the "family prayer" idea would pass. Instead, Janet asked me, "Carol, when is the best time for you to pray? I know you are probably the busiest of all of us."

I said, "Don't arrange it around me. Just go ahead even if I can't come."

"Oh no, Carol," Julie, one of my new roommates, insisted. "We can't have it without you! It's not the same unless everyone is there."

"Okay." I gave in. "How about right before dinner?" I hoped to combine family prayer with the blessing at dinner.

"I really think we should pray first thing in the morning," said Wendy, who was from Salt Lake City. "It would start our day off right."

Sharon, my old friend from Phoenix, said, "But I leave early in the morning to go practice French horn in the fine arts center. I'm usually there by 6:00 a.m." Sharon was a more diligent musician than I.

"Oh, so we will have to pray at about 5:45, won't we?" Janet said.

I couldn't believe she was serious.

"That wouldn't be so bad," said Becky, also from Salt Lake City. "Some of us could just go back to bed."

"Okay, let's start tomorrow morning. I'll lead it," said Janet.

The next morning a gentle hand on my shoulder awakened me. "Carol," whispered Sharon, "It's a quarter 'til six. Time for prayer."

I stumbled out of bed into the kitchen to find everyone else, looking just as sleepy as I felt, kneeling on the floor. I sat on a chair, bowed my head, and my eyes fell shut.

"Let's all kneel as we pray," said Janet.

Grudgingly I obliged. "Why am I doing this?" I thought. "Maybe I need to find some new roommates."

"Our dear heavenly Father," Janet began, "we thy daughters come before thee humbly this morning to ask thy blessing upon us this day. We ask thee to bless us in our daily lives and in our schoolwork so that we may do well and be pleasing unto thee.

"Heavenly Father, we also beseech thee on behalf of the leadership of this thy Church. We know the great responsibility thou hast placed on them, and we ask thee to strengthen our Prophet and give him physical health and wisdom to speak thy word."

Janet prayed on for the apostles and missionaries. Then she said, "Father, now we would ask thee to open the eyes and hearts of those who have not seen the light of the everlasting gospel. We pray that you would remove the veil from their minds, and they would realize and accept the truth of thy Church. We know this is thy plan for our exaltation and our return to thy presence. We say these things in the name of thy Son, Jesus Christ. Amen."

"Amen," echoed everyone. So began our day.

That afternoon, Becky stuck her head into my room while I was studying. "Carol," she said, "I hope we don't impose on you too much, since you're not LDS. If I were you, I would feel sort of intimidated. We just want you to see the truth of the gospel because we care so much about you."

"I know you do, Becky. Thanks for saying that."

Before she left she said, "I know how I would feel in your shoes. Pretty alone sometimes."

It was easy to love Becky.

Janet took a different approach. She put a five-page letter on my dresser the next day. In it, Janet told me again that she knew the Church was true, and she pleaded with me to pray with an open mind and ask the Holy Ghost to reveal the truth to me. She expressed her concern for me (which I knew was genuine), and said that she would be accountable before God if she did not tell me these things. She asked me not to rush to my Baptist friends with this challenge but to accept it from her and from God openly. She promised that if I found the Church to be untrue, she and three and one-half million Saints would leave the Church.[3]

Dear Janet! She had been such a faithful friend to me, such a kind, thoughtful roommate. How could I respond to such a letter? I was not angry or resentful—I was troubled. I thought seriously about her challenge to investigate the Church. Had I really asked God to show me the truth?

The next day Janet was alone in her room. I entered, sat on her bed, and said, "Janet, thank you for that letter. I know it comes from a sincere heart."

She looked at me with relief in her eyes. "Oh, Carol," she said, "I hope it didn't make you mad. I really had to write that. I knew I was responsible to God and had to put the responsibility on you. I don't want to be blamed if you miss eternal salvation. Please consider what I said. Come talk with me anytime about it."

On the weekend, while I was ironing in the laundry room, Brother Calkins came in. Brother Calkins and his wife, Sister Calkins, were the head residents of our apartment building. He knew I was a Gentile.

He casually walked over to where I was ironing. "I noticed on your housing application form that you are not a member of the Church. That's very interesting."

"Yes, it is," I agreed. "There aren't many non-members around here."

He said, "I wasn't raised in the Church. I used to be a Nazarene, and didn't find any meaning there, so later I became a Catholic. That didn't work out either, and then through a series of miraculous events, I found the Church. It has really changed my life."

I responded by sharing my own testimony. "I myself wasn't raised as a Christian. About two years ago Christ came into my life. I've changed a lot also."

We continued talking, but we just weren't connecting. Finally Brother Calkins said, "Carol, you are going to join the Church. All good people do."

What could I say to that? I stood there in silence. After a moment he smiled and said, "Well, I'd better let you get back to your ironing."

After Brother Calkins left, I ironed with a vengeance. "Why don't people just leave me alone?" I wondered. "They say they care about me. But I sure get tired of hearing about Mormonism."

I suddenly thought, "What if it really is true? I've never honestly accepted the challenge to 'ask God if these things are true' as they always say."

I put away my ironing and wandered the campus. I had come to BYU with the notion that Mormonism was false. I knew that only one religion—Mormonism or Christianity—could be true; not both. I had to choose. Was I afraid to ask God to show me which to choose, as Joseph Smith had done?

"Wait a minute," I said to myself, "this is ridiculous. You're the president of the Baptist Student Union. Not only that, but God has done so much in your life, especially since you've been at BYU. You didn't dream up all those miracles. Don't submit to this whim of the moment."

The words of Janet's letter came to my mind. "I promise you, dear sister, that if you will pray to God with an open mind and ask Him if what I have said is true, you will have a good feeling come over you and the Holy Ghost will bear witness to its truthfulness. . . .I also guarantee that you will never rest the same if you deny the feelings you receive. . . .Now the weight is on you to test it and prove it to yourself."

"All right, all right. Lord," I prayed, "I feel silly after all this time here, coming to ask you if the Mormon Church is true, but I have to be honest about it. And I know that if you reveal to me that it is true, I'll have to obey the truth and join the Church. I put myself in your hands because I love you and want to be exactly where you want me to be. Thank you that I can trust you. Amen."

I stopped to listen to God's Spirit. His presence was very real as these thoughts came to me:

"Carol, you don't need to ask for the 'burning in the bosom.' Your faith is based on facts. Use your head, not your bosom. Read the Bible. Jesus was my final word. He died and rose from the dead so that you could have life. That's all you need. There is no new gospel."[4]

Notes:
[1] An engineer later told me it was because the tires expanded due to the heat generated by driving.
[2] Temple garments are special undergarments worn by Latter-day Saints who have been through the temple ceremonies. The garments, marked with special symbols, remind wearers of the vows they made in the temple, primarily the vow not to reveal what they saw and heard there. Originally, these garments were thought to protect the wearer from harm.
[3] There are now more than six and a half million members in the Mormon Church.
[4] See the appendix for a list of resources that examine the authenticity of Mormonism and historical Christianity.

Chapter Eight

One Sunday, before the evening church service, a lady hurried up to me and said, "Carol, a new college student just walked in. Come meet him."

As I approached him, the student said, "Hi, my name is Tom Murphy. I was just riding by and saw some action here so I stopped in. I'm a student at the 'Y'."

"So am I. Are you Baptist?"

"No." Tom hesitated. "In fact, I'm a Mormon right now. I hope I'm still welcome."

"Of course." I wondered about Tom being a Mormon "right now." I introduced Tom to Dawnena, and after chuch we invited him to join us for a snack and conversation. Over French fries and a Dr. Pepper, he told us his story.

"I was raised in a Christian home. I never appreciated it. I accepted Christ as a child but I just coasted along—I took it all for granted. Then, in high school, I met a Mormon girl who talked constantly about her church. She wanted me to investigate it, but my parents wouldn't hear of it. Last year I finally took the lessons that the missionaries teach. At first, what they said sounded strange, but it seemed logical. The elders had an answer for every question I raised. They proved their case; I didn't have any more objections, so I was baptized.

"When I joined the LDS Church my parents were grieved. In order to get away from home, I decided to come to Provo for school. I like the school, but the more I study religion here, the more I begin to doubt the Church.

"Then I read the *Journal of Discourses*—a collection of sermons. I was amazed. Have you heard of the doctrine of blood atonement? I read in one of Brigham Young's sermons that Christ's death didn't pay for some sins. People who commit those sins can only be forgiven if their own blood is shed.[1] In fact, according to the law in Utah, criminals are still executed by firing squad, so that their blood is shed."

Dawnena said, "The book of Hebrews says that if Jesus didn't die for every sin, then He didn't die for any. Christ's sacrifice was once for all."[2]

"I know. I remember that from my childhood Sunday School class. In the *Discourses*, I read that these sins were adultery, wizardry, and even drunkenness. I also read about Adam being God. It said he came down into Eden with Eve, one of his celestial wives. And it said Adam was Michael the Archangel, the Ancient of Days, and that he was our God, the only God with whom we have to do.[3] There were other strange ideas, too. You should read them sometime.

"Anyway, the Lord opened my eyes, and I felt foolish for having gotten into the Church. But it is hard to leave the Church when you live in Provo and attend BYU. I have five housemates—all returned missionaries. They know I don't attend the student branch anymore, and they harass me about it. By the way, if you ever call my house, don't tell them you're from the Baptist church. I have enough problems."

I looked at Dawnena. She looked at Tom and back at me. We sat in silence for a moment. Then she said, "Why don't you transfer to another university?"

"I've already applied to a Christian school in Oklahoma."

Tom did finish the semester at BYU and left for Oklahoma. Though our acquaintance was brief, his story encouraged us for a long time. After a hard day, we'd think of Tom and remind ourselves, "The Lord knows who are His" (II Timothy 2:19).

The Sunday after Tom's first visit, another visitor attended First Baptist Church. A handsome friend of mine, David Monson, had recently returned from a mission in Uruguay, and we shared several music classes. When he entered, I remembered a conversation we'd had earlier in the week.

It was Monday afternoon, and as we packed up our instruments after an orchestra rehearsal, David remarked, "I have to teach Family Home Evening tonight. I'm not prepared. . . .Carol, do you teach sometimes, too?"

"I used to," I replied, "but I don't go to Family Home Evening anymore."

"You don't? Shame on you. Why not?"

"I'm not LDS."

"I didn't know that." With a piece of his clarinet in each hand, David paused and looked hard at me. I felt as though he were trying to read my soul. "May I ask what you are?"

"I'm a Christian. I go to the Baptist church."

David put the pieces of his clarinet away and closed his locker thoughtfully. "I would like to come visit your church. My meeting ends at 5 p.m. on Sundays. Does your church hold evening meetings?"

"Yes, at six o'clock."

He said, "Give me the address of your church. I'll probably call you if I decide to come."

Our conversation had slipped my mind until he rolled

into the church parking lot on his bicycle. David didn't criticize the service. He participated in and seemed to enjoy the worship, and I enjoyed talking with him. His gentle attitude impressed me. He appeared genuinely interested.

I saw him daily in my classes, and we began studying together. Often during our discussions of music theory my eyes were drawn from the book to David's handsome profile. Thoughts of him lingered in my head long after I'd forgotten the facts we'd studied. I wanted to keep my thoughts and feelings secret. Too late I realized what was happening to me. I was falling in love with David.

Now I was afraid. This was serious. A romance with a returned missionary could only lead to trouble. Many women I knew had joined the Church under the influence of romantic love. I was headed for Mormonism, or I was headed for heartache.

But my heart was naive and unreasonable. David's cheerful, "Hello, Carol," brightened my days, and long orchestra rehearsals passed quickly as I listened to David lead the clarinet section. Often I caught him looking my way, and always we'd turn quickly back to our music.

The LDS Church is authoritative with young people about dating relationships. A faithful Mormon does not marry outside the Church, and because "every date is a potential mate," he or she does not date outside the Church. David's devotion to the Church and its principles meant he would not date me. But we were drawn to each other.

I remembered the comment of a Christian girl who came to BYU and left within a semester. She said, "I feel like some kind of social reject. I haven't been out on a date since I came here."

"Don't take it personally," I remarked wryly, "but I

know what you mean. It's 'water, water, everywhere, and not a drop to drink'."

Now I could almost taste the water. It was agony.

The fall semester was nearly finished, and I desperately wanted to flee the scene and collect my thoughts. I fled the scene—but my feelings for David came with me to Phoenix for the Christmas holidays. Every time I thought of him, the Holy Spirit compassionately reminded me of Jesus—my first love.

I returned to school in January with a resolve to conquer my emotions. By sheer discipline, I told myself, I would get this wonderful, handsome Mormon out of my heart, and my life would be back to normal.

I first saw David in the bookstore. The moment he smiled at me all my resolve disappeared. The next weeks became a cycle of resolutions, failures, repentances, confessions, and new resolutions. Why did we have to have so many classes together? I considered changing my schedule.

Although I prayed day and night about it, I was trying in my own strength to do right. And, secretly, I enjoyed every moment with David, every glance, every word. I knew that if I truly gave my heart to God, He would change me.

Whenever I rebel in some area of my life, I lose spiritual power. So it came as no surprise when I began to lose the vitality that comes from a close walk with God. My devotional life dried up. I lost interest in other people. Nothing mattered but the moments I shared with David. I knew I was in rebellion, yet my heart clung tenaciously to its desires.

One Sunday late in January my loving, firm counselor—the Holy Spirit—intervened. The sermon was about people who tell God to leave them alone. It made my heart ache. The words of the hymn we sang in the morning service rang in my head all afternoon:

*All to Jesus I surrender,
All to Him I freely give.
I will ever love and trust Him,
In His presence daily live.
I surrender all.
All to Jesus, Precious Savior,
I surrender all.*

"Oh, Lord," I prayed, "I *am* sorry. I know you're right and I'm wrong. I have to give this up. I'm tired of fighting my feelings. Every time I think of David my heart skips, and then it aches terribly. I know I am disobeying you.

"Thank you for being patient with me. Now I am ready to lay my friendship with David in your hands, and I want you to have your way with me. Please help me to be tenderhearted and to follow you. Even now as I think of him, I ache inside. You have a big miracle to work in my heart. Please, please help me. Thank you so much. In Jesus' name."

Even after I asked God's help, I didn't believe the problem would simply disappear. I woke up the next morning braced for another day of fighting my feelings. But the feelings were gone. I thought about David during the day (especially when I saw him) but the heaviness and longing had disappeared.

I was also pleasantly surprised by something else. My feelings had changed, but I wondered how I should respond to David. I didn't want to hurt him, but before I could speak with him, I noticed that his attitude had changed, too. Overnight we had become colleagues—the romantic flames had been quenched. There was no earthly explanation for David's coinciding change of heart.

After that, what remained in me was a tender memory of David, and of the Lord's faithfulness in healing me when I gave my heart to Him.

During that fall, Don Plott had moved to another church, so First Baptist was without a pastor. A spirit of cooperation prevailed as the laymen adeptly carried on the ministry. A pulpit committee began to search for our new minister. They brought prospective pastors before the congregation, and finally accepted a young man from Texas, Phil McKown. Phil and his wife and daughter moved to Provo soon after. We were grateful to God for bringing a man who knew the Scriptures well; in Provo it helped to know the Bible.

After Phil was settled in Provo, I offered to take him on a tour of BYU. We walked the campus together and stopped in at the Wilkinson Center. Phil suggested, "Let's sit down and talk about the BSU. Where can we get a cup of coffee?"

I smiled and said, "Not here."

"Oh, that's right. I keep forgetting. What do people drink around here?"

"Root beer, orange soda, fruit punch, hot chocolate—anything the Church says is free of caffeine."

We found a table, and I told Phil the story of the Baptist Student Union.

"It seems to me," he said after listening, "that there must be some way to reach those students who aren't Mormon. Maybe you can get those lists of Baptist students earlier than October. I've been thinking; there are several matters I would like to speak with the university president about. What's his name again, Oaks or something?"

"Yes, Dallin Oaks."

"I want to get to know him."

Then Phil changed the subject. "Carol, are you planning to stay here until you graduate?"

"I don't know yet." Phil had asked a question that had been weighing heavily on my mind. "I've been thinking about transferring to another school."

"Do you like it here?"

I thought for a moment. "At first I didn't. It takes a while to get used to this place. But now I like it. On the other hand, I'd like to find out what life is like at a secular school. And, I'm not sure I want a degree from BYU because I may go into full-time Christian work."

"You don't want a degree from Brigham Young University on your resume?" Phil laughed. "I can understand that. Where would you transfer to?"

"I've been thinking about the music school at North Texas State University. It's outstanding, and it would be a relief to live in the Bible Belt for a change."

Phil had an appointment and I had a class, so we parted ways. But our conversation provoked my thoughts. Did I really want to leave BYU? I was pleased with my studies—the academic environment at BYU was excellent. I saw the Lord at work in my life and in the Baptist Student Union.

In fact, the BSU was becoming famous. My sister, Nancy, now a high school senior, visited a BYU recruiter's meeting just as I had two years earlier. However, this time the recruiter had added to his speech: "And for all you non-Mormons, we have an active Baptist student organization at BYU."

When I heard this, I laughed with delight. The university was publicizing the Baptist Student Union!

But as much as I delighted in the ministry at BYU, my

desire to apply to North Texas State persisted. I submitted an application and competed for music scholarships. Because out-of-state tuition rates were high, I needed a scholarship to waive those rates. Once again, I waited and trusted the Lord to guide me by providing, or by taking away the desire to leave. Meanwhile, I resolved to make the most of every moment at BYU as though it were my last.

Not long afterward, I was at home in our apartment and heard a knock on the door. Two young men in dark suits were waiting when I opened the door. I was startled when one said, "We'd like to speak with Carol Avery."

"I'm Carol. Are you the new missionaries on campus?" I had recently heard that, for the first time, a team of full-time missionaries would be assigned to proselytize the non-Mormon students at BYU.

"Yes, we are. May we come in?"

"Certainly." I offered the men seats in the living room, and I noticed that a couple of my roommates had slipped in to see what was happening. In a moment, the senior missionary got down to business and invited me to take the set of discussions.

Scenes of my last encounter with the missionaries passed through my mind. But now I was a different person. I had talked with so many returned missionaries that I was sure I'd heard all they had to say. A trip through missionary lessons would be a valuable experience now. Besides, many of my friends had challenged me to take the lessons and perhaps now, before I left, I could pacify them.

I answered, "I'd like to take the lessons, but I'm too busy right now. If you check back in a few weeks, I'll have more time." I was sure they wouldn't forget to return.

That spring, the student government elections presented one more challenge for me. The editorial section of the *Daily Universe*, the school paper, was full of letters about one particular candidate—a Black student. Never before had any Black been elected to office at BYU. Robert Lee Stevenson, the vice-presidential running mate of Randy Sloat, was truly a novelty.

When Janet heard of his campaign, she told me the inside scoop. "I knew Bob Stevenson in Germany when my father was stationed there. Bob was a soldier. He used to be Baptist, but he joined the Church while in Germany. He told me back then that he would attend BYU and run for office. I think this is the Lord's will. Of course, because he is Black, Bob cannot hold the priesthood or serve a mission, but he is an outstanding man, and he can serve the Church in this way."

I asked Victor if he knew Bob.

He answered, "Of course. And you know what I think? This school is going to elect him just to prove they aren't prejudiced. Wait and see."

When the election results were in, the Sloat and Stevenson team won by a considerable margin.

I wanted to meet this character. While walking between classes one day, I saw Victor and Bob coming in my direction. As I approached, Victor introduced me.

"Bob, this is Carol Avery. Carol, have you met Bob Stevenson?"

"No, I haven't. Bob, I've looked forward to meeting you. I think you know one of my roommates, Janet Merrill."

"Yes, she was in Germany when I was stationed there."

Victor said, "Carol is the president of the Baptist Student Union."

Bob took a step backward. "Are you putting me on? How can you live here and still be Baptist? The Church is true—if you can't see it here, you won't see it anywhere."

I answered, "Yes, I think you're right. If the Church is true, I couldn't miss it living here. But, Bob, I don't see how you could join the Mormon Church after being Baptist, if you were truly a Christian."

Bob began to defend the Mormon Church vigorously. His experience in a Baptist church, he said, had proven to him how wrong apostate Christianity was.

I realized that our discussion was unreasonable, and I worked toward ending it. Bob seemed willing to orate for hours, but I finally slipped away, glad to say I was almost late for class. I shivered as I left the scene. Bob was misinformed and outspoken about Christianity, and I knew the Mormon media would take advantage of every word he said.

The Baptist Student Union had arranged for a team of five students from Howard Payne University in Brownwood, Texas to spend their spring break at BYU. The National Student Ministries of the Southern Baptist Convention often sent Help Teams on short-term mission projects, but until now, no one had dreamed of coming to Brigham Young University.

Diane and I saw great potential for a week of help from five enthusiastic students from Texas. We planned for them to spend most of their time visiting international students and distributing Gideon New Testaments. Diane had obtained permission for the team to distribute Bibles in the Student Center. We wanted the Texas students to experience life in Utah, so we arranged for them to attend the weekly BYU devotional and to take a trip to Temple Square in Salt Lake City.

When they arrived, the students tumbled out of a large

Living with the Latter-day Saints

black sedan into our Sunday evening worship service. I was secretly pleased that one of the team members, John, was a Black. We told him of the recent controversial election, and he chuckled as he read a related newspaper clipping.

The team members, paired off with our BSU students, visited in dozens of internationals' homes, delivering New Testaments and sharing Christ. The internationals, many of them non-Mormons, received us well. Some even joined us for a mid-week Bible study.

Thursday morning was the time we had set for distributing Bibles in the Wilkinson Center. I admired the spunk of the Help Team members who were enthusiastic about handing out Scripture to hundreds of Mormons. I was sorry to miss out on the excitement because of an important class. But I heard the story later.

Many of the students were polite and willing to engage in conversation, and one returned with a Book of Mormon for the team member who had given him a Bible. Then, after most of the Bibles had been distributed, a university administrator approached the team with a determined gleam in his eye. The team members stopped short.

"Who are you," he demanded, "and why are you distributing literature on our campus?"

Tom, the team leader, said, "We are with the Baptist Student Union, and we were told that we had university approval to hand out these New Testaments here today."

"I don't know anything about that. Where is the faculty sponsor of this group? Who is in charge of this?"

"I'm sorry, but the sponsor of the Baptist Student

Union is teaching and the president is in class," Tom said politely.

"You will stop handing out these materials and come with me right now."

John, the Black student, spoke up. "Sir, some of us have an important appointment at 11 o'clock. May I go with you myself so the others will not miss their interview?"

The administrator fixed a stare on each student in turn and finally consented to take John in and release the others. It was after 10 o'clock already and the four remaining members of the team hurried off to find the KBYU television studios where Victor Hogstrom had arranged for an interview on his program, "Religion Today."

As they waited for Tom's five-minute interview to begin, the team anxiously discussed John's fate in the administration building. My class over, I rushed to the studio to cheer Tom on and caught the last of their panicked story.

"...and the guy took John with him, and we haven't seen him since!"

A voice behind me said, "Here I am." We all turned to see John saunter up with a gigantic grin on his face. "It's cool."

"What happened?" We couldn't pull the story out of him fast enough.

"I tell you, that guy was mad. He insisted over and over that this was a private institution, and we had no right to be here. University policy prohibits distribution of tracts, he said. Well, I explained that we had gotten permission from that—um, what's it called again, Carol—oh yeah, the Associated Students of BYU, to do what we were doing. After a while he cooled off, and I promised we wouldn't give out any more Bibles. Of course, we were almost finished anyway. That was all. He let me go. But I thought these guys believe the Bible. Why are they afraid of us, five little guys handing out Scripture?"

Victor joined us. "Tom, you're on camera in seven minutes, right after a couple of news items."

"Okay. Thanks, Victor," Tom said. "Whew, I'm a little nervous."

I told him, "There's nothing to it. I had an interview just like this last year. We're all praying for you." It was fun to sound experienced.

"Thanks. Here I go." Tom was escorted to a seat under the lights. His interviewer asked about the work of the Baptist Student Union and about the Help Team. Tom answered each question coherently. At one point he mentioned his conversion to Christ, and the interviewer, following the lead, asked Tom what he meant by "conversion to Christ."

Without hesitation, Tom answered, "I was converted to Christ, that is, I became a Christian when I asked Christ to control my life. It's more than simply knowing *about* Jesus Christ. I had to come to the place of admitting my sin, inadequacy, and need for God. Because of the death and resurrection of Jesus Christ, we can be forgiven and have a personal relationship with God."

Tom paused for a breath. The cameraman was signaling wildly to wind up the interview. The interviewer said, "Thank you very much, Tom Jackson, for being part of *Religion Today*." The camera moved quickly back to the anchorman for more news.

I took Friday off from school to join the team as they went to Temple Square in Salt Lake City. Non-Mormons are not allowed to enter the temple itself, but the elaborate visitors center on the temple grounds provided movies and guided tours for guests. We arrived at the Temple in time to join a guided tour, which included a walk around the complex and a look inside the Mormon Tabernacle, a large auditorium with unusually live acoustics.

In the visitors center, the guides told the story of the angels Moroni and Mormon, of Christ's visit to the Americas, the appearance of the Father and the Son to Joseph Smith, and the Restoration of the True Church and the Priesthood in the latter days.

One of the girls from Texas whispered in my ear, "This is nothing but fairy tales!"

I concealed a smile. "If you knew nothing about the Bible, it would sound logical to you. The Mormon Church explains why many Protestant and Catholic churches are dry and dead—because the True Church ceased to exist when the last apostle died. If a dry, dead church had been your experience, you'd look into the Mormon Church, too."

We returned to Provo, and the next morning, the students packed themselves and their luggage into the black sedan and drove back to Texas.

In the coming days and weeks though, I noticed some remarkable changes in our Baptist Student Union. The Help Team had ignited sparks of enthusiasm among our students. Our weekly meeting became vibrant Bible studies, and students who hadn't attended often came more regularly. Diane and I began to delegate responsibilities to other students, which not only lightened our load but also spread out the ownership of the BSU.

We even began publishing a monthly newsletter. One evening Dawnena, the editor, called me. "Miss President," she said, "the deadline for the newsletter is tomorrow. I want to know what you'd like to say in the 'President's Column'."

I laughed with delight. "You mean I have my own

column? How important that sounds! When do I move into the Oval Office?"

"One thing at a time," she chided. "Seriously, I want to include a president's message in each issue. Write something up and give it to me tomorrow morning."

I said, "I'll be glad to. Thanks a lot."

I hung up the phone, sat back, and smiled. God had done marvelous things among us. I knew we were God's people, in God's place, at God's time.

Notes:
[1] Blood atonement is taught in the *Journal of Discourses*, Volume 4, pages 53-54.
[2] See Hebrews 7:27 and chapters 9-10.
[3] *Journal of Discourses*, Volume 1, pp. 50-51. Today's Mormon Church leaders do not accept the "Adam-God doctrine," although at least one Apostle, Bruce R. McConkie, admits that Brigham Young did teach it.

Chapter Nine

Most of my roommates were staying for summer school, but our university apartment had to be vacated for incoming missionaries studying at the Language Training Mission. So on top of exams, we spent the last weeks of the spring semester cleaning, moving, and cleaning some more. We had been transferred to another building in the complex and settled in just as school began again.

Life was more relaxed in the summer. As the temperatures rose, we looked for every excuse to study outdoors, have picnics, or play frisbee. Some of the regular school activities were discontinued for the summer, leaving us more leisure time.

One afternoon during the first week of classes, Becky met me as I walked in the door. "Oh, Carol," she said, "The Mission Mormonaries came by to see you."

I looked at her in surprise. "Who?" I asked.

"The Mission Mormonaries from the Church of Cheese and Crackers of Rattle-day Snakes," she laughed. "When my brother was on his mission, we used to call him that."

"Oh. What did the elders say?" I was afraid to call the missionaries by that name.

"They'll call back."

Later that day the phone rang. "Carol, this is Elder Smith. Did your roommate tell you we stopped by?"

"Yes."

"Is there anything we can do for you today?"

"I can't think of anything."

"Carol, we'd like to begin the discussions about the Church with you. Are you free tomorrow?"

"Yes, around lunchtime." I was looking forward to starting the program.

Elder Smith said, "Twelve o'clock would be perfect. We'll see you in the lobby of your apartment building."

Promptly at noon the next day, the dark-suited elders arrived. Each shook my hand firmly, and we sat in the lobby. After they chatted for awhile—and asked me again if there was anything they could do for me today—we delved into the first lesson. Using a ring-bound notebook filled with illustrations, the elders took turns explaining the Restoration of the Church and the testimony of Joseph Smith.[1]

During the discussion, the elders asked me several leading questions. For example, as one elder explained the importance of prophets in the Old Testament, he asked, "Carol, why do you feel it would be helpful for God to give us direction and help today?" The question, in context, presupposes that God gives direction only through prophets.

"Our message and testimony to you is that God continues to guide His children today through living prophets. Our church is organized as Ephesians chapter four directs with apostles and prophets."

The elders gave me a pamphlet containing the testimony of Joseph Smith. One explained that Christ told Joseph Smith in a vision to join none of the churches, for they all taught the doctrines of men and not of God.

Then he asked me, "Does this help you understand why the churches today teach so many conflicting doctrines?"

I was supposed to say, "Yes, because the churches teach the doctrines of men."

Instead of giving them the answer they wanted, I said, "The Bible-believing churches don't teach many conflicting doctrines, they only vary on minor points."

The men just went on to explain that the *Book of Mormon* is God's gift to us, given to clarify and add to the Bible. Then they told me about the priesthood that the apostles Peter, James, and John gave to Joseph Smith in another vision. They told me that that priesthood had passed from Joseph Smith through a succession of apostles and prophets to the present day. Then they explained that because of the Restoration of the Church, I could now receive the full blessings of the Kingdom of God.

I said, "Wait a minute! I *have* received the blessings of God. I don't need an external structure or the *Book of Mormon* to receive them. Because of Jesus Christ, I have access to God."

The missionaries smiled. Written on their faces was their condescending opinion of my unenlightened mind. They reviewed the concepts of the lesson, tried to clarify what they had said, and asked me questions such as, "Can you accept the fact that Joseph Smith received from an angel the gold plates on which the *Book of Mormon* was written?" and "How do you feel that knowing there is a living prophet on the earth today will help your family?"

The elders closed the meeting by promising me that I would know for certain the truth of these things through sincere prayer. Elder Tanner explained to me the "formula" for prayer. I was to begin with "Our Father in heaven," then thank Him for my blessings, ask for the things I need, and close in the name of Jesus Christ. He then knelt down and asked me to lead a closing prayer. I could tell by the way he said it that he thought I had never in my life prayed aloud.

After I prayed, Elder Smith got up from his knees and said, "That was a beautiful prayer. We know that as you continue to pray sincerely the Lord will answer your prayers."

He reminded me to study the pamphlet about Joseph Smith and look up several passages in the *Book of Mormon* before our meeting next week.

After they left I thought, "That wasn't so bad. If I can be honest with them and not get defensive, I think we will get along fine."

I diligently did my homework during the week. Ironically, the more I read the *Book of Mormon*, the weaker it sounded. It was a poor imitation of the King James Bible.

Janet walked in carrying the mail. "Carol, here's a letter from North Texas State University."

I had received several letters from the university, but no news about scholarships. I was tired of waiting and wondering. I tore into the envelope to find a letter that read, "Dear Miss Avery: We are pleased to inform you that you have been selected as the recipient of an academic scholarship."

The letter explained that my out-of-state tuition would also be waived.

I scrambled for a pen to sign the acceptance form. Before I mailed it in, I called Diane to tell her the news. We both hated the thought of parting. I was relieved when she responded with a sincere, "Praise the Lord. I know He's doing His perfect will in your life."

The next day I stopped in to tell a favorite music professor about my scholarship. He congratulated me and expressed his disappointment that I was leaving BYU. I also mentioned that I had begun taking the missionary lessons.

My professor knew that I was a Christian. To my surprise he—a Latter-day Saint—leaned forward in his chair and asked me, "What are you doing that for?"

"Well," I hesitated, "why not? People have been after me for two years to take them, so I decided to do it while I'm here."

"The lessons are designed to lead investigators into the Church. Tell me what you think of them. And remember, curiosity killed the cat."

My second session with the elders dealt with eternal progression—the belief that we lived in heaven as spirits before we came to be mortals on earth, and we are here to get a body of flesh and bone and to be tested. Eternal progression also meant that "as man is, God once was; as God is, man may become."

We also discussed salvation by baptism, and baptism for the dead. Again I was disturbed by the structure of the questions, which often led me to answer according to their script. A discussion about whether baptism was essential to salvation ensued. The missionaries were convinced that it was, and I maintained that faith alone saved us.

Elder Smith had the last word. "Carol, this is another concept that you will come to understand only by prayer and study."

As the elders left, I impulsively asked, "Would you like to stay for dinner next week?"

They exchanged glances and said, "We'd love to."

When I told my roommates what I had done, they were delighted. For them it was a privilege to entertain missionaries, the defenders of the faith and heroes to any BYU coed.

On Thursday I prepared enchiladas and left Sharon to watch the oven during my lesson. This third session was not as filled with doctrine as the first two. We talked about "continuing revelation," which the Mormons believe comes today through their Prophet and Apostles and through Latter-day Scriptures—the *Book of Mormon*, the *Doctrine and Covenants*, and the *Pearl of Great Price*. The elders taught that all authority and knowledge necessary for salvation are found in the Church of Jesus Christ of Latter-day Saints, and they emphasized the importance of complete obedience to Church leaders.

When the elders spoke of the Church of Jesus Christ of Latter-day Saints, they often omitted the phrase "of Latter-day Saints." Each time they did, I felt more irritated. I finally said, "I've noticed you don't always distinguish between the Church of Jesus Christ and the LDS Church. I am a member of the Church of Jesus Christ. I am not a member of the Church of Jesus Christ of Latter-day Saints."

I paused, feeling better for having spoken my mind. But now I sensed tension in the air. I softened and said, "Go ahead with what you were saying."

The men exchanged glances. They didn't respond but picked up where they had left off in the black picture notebook.

The third lesson over, we broke for dinner. As I served the meal, Janet engaged the missionaries in conversation, and soon all my roommates were helping my guests feel at home.

We had a relaxed and light-hearted evening. After a couple of hours, they left for an evening appointment.

Sharon helped with the dishes. She said, "You're lucky to be taking the discussions with those elders. Are you learning a lot?"

"Mostly I'm learning how they present the Church to investigators. I already knew a lot about Mormonism."

"I suppose so. I hope you take what the elders say seriously."

Lesson Four was entitled "Truth *versus* Error." After they established the importance of truth, the elders taught that God's truth all but disappeared from the earth after the last apostle died. As always, one of the elders referred to a Bible verse that seemed to support their view. This time it was, "For the time will come when they will not endure sound doctrine; but after their own lusts shall they heap to themselves teachers, having itching ears; and they shall turn away their ears from the truth, and shall be turned unto fables" (II Timothy 4:3-4, KJV).

I protested. "Just because some people turned away from sound doctrine doesn't mean the church was lost from the earth. The verse doesn't say everyone will go astray."

"We believe God came and restored the Church through Joseph Smith because man had gone astray, and the True Church was lost from the earth," said one elder. "By the way, Carol, how do you feel now about Joseph Smith and his vision of God?"

I answered, "I can never believe He appeared to Joseph Smith. The Bible teaches that God is spirit. No one has seen God."

I could tell that my teachers were getting frustrated. They hadn't—in four lessons—convinced me even to believe that God has a body of flesh and bone. Finally one elder said, "You still don't believe in the three-in-one doctrine, do you?"

"In the Trinity? Yes, I do."

"Carol, haven't you seen all those verses about the face of God and His hands and arms? Don't you know He created man in His image? And how could Jesus be on earth and be God in heaven at the same time? How could God pray to Himself?" We had departed from the memorized outline.

"I could show you verses that say God is spirit, and that no man can see God. I could also show you where the Bible says God became a man in Jesus. I can't fully understand it, but I do believe it," I answered calmly.

Elder Smith said, "Carol, what can we do to help you see God is not three-in-one?"

"Nothing."

The other elder picked up where he had left off in the discussion and began talking about the LDS plan of salvation. The first point, faith, was refreshingly common ground. The elders were relieved that I agreed with them on the importance of faith. I also liked their second point, repentance, until they said that if the sin were ever repeated, the repentance was invalid.

I also had trouble with point three in the plan—that baptism is essential to salvation. On the fourth and last principle—the "laying on of hands," we ran completely aground. The elders explained that after a new convert is baptized, the missionaries lay their hands on him or her and bestow the gift of the Holy Ghost.

Elder Tanner asked me, "Do you feel the gift of the Holy Ghost is a blessing worth working for?"

"Worth working for?" I exclaimed. "How can you work for a gift? You just said the Holy Ghost is a gift. The Holy Ghost is in my life, but I didn't work to get Him. And no one laid their hands on me so I would receive Him."

As we neared the end of the lesson, Elder Smith mentioned the importance of goals. After challenging me to set goals in my personal life, he suggested a specific date at the end of the month by which I should know for certain the truth of the Church. I noticed later that the date was a Saturday on which baptisms were held.

I thought, "So this is the challenge to join the Church. I wondered when this was coming."

I dropped into my music professor's office again. He asked, "How are your missionary lessons going?"

"We have our ups and downs," I said gloomily. "This last discussion was trying."

"In what way?" he asked.

"The elders are frustrated with me because I don't agree with them on the most basic points. I'm frustrated because I don't want to be obnoxious, but I'm not willing to compromise what I believe."

"I see." He waited to see whether I had more to say, then spoke again. "I joined the Church after missionary age so I never served a full-time mission, but I've worked as a stake missionary to teach investigators. I always tried to beef up the lessons because I wanted to present an accurate picture of the Church, not just convince people to join it. I think the emphasis of the lessons might be misleading."

"I'm glad to hear you say that." My respect for this professor increased every time I talked with him. And I approached the fifth lesson much encouraged.

The emphasis of the fifth lesson changed from doctrine to practice. This time we went over the commandments. The principle behind obedience, said the elders, was that "the commandments of God are given to show us how to achieve eternal life and become like God."

First was the law of tithing. Although I didn't consider tithing a "law," I had made a practice of tithing since I'd become a Christian. When I told the elders, they were astonished. They praised my "good works" and went on to the second point.

We agreed about the law of chastity. It was Elder Tanner's turn to talk, and I could see he was glad to be spared from giving a discourse on the evils of immorality.

The next point was the Word of Wisdom. The other elder asked me pointedly whether I used tobacco, alcoholic beverages, coffee, or tea.

I answered honestly. "I drink tea when I'm at home, but I don't drink it on campus. I signed the Code of Honor when I came to BYU."

Elder Smith delivered a short sermon on the evils of tea, and said, "You're fortunate to have the example of others around you who maintain the Word of Wisdom."

Next we talked about the Sabbath. I knew that nearly every store and restaurant in Utah was closed on Sunday, and that many Mormons even frowned on going on picnics and participating in sports on Sundays. As one elder explained, we should avoid activities—such as sports, picnics, and household duties—that detract from the spirit of the day.

I didn't agree. I'd observed my roommates, who kept the letter of the law by studying only religion or writing letters on Sundays, but missed the spirit of the law. For them, Sunday wasn't a day of rest. I read from Mark 2:27, "The Sabbath was made for man, not man for the Sabbath."

The elders grudgingly agreed that picnicking on Sundays probably would not keep anyone out of the Celestial Kingdom.

By the end of this lesson, I realized that Mormons and Christians did the same things but for different reasons. Latter-day Saints follow God's guidelines as a set of commandments which, when they are obeyed, earn favor in God's sight and entitled them to God's blessings and praise. I viewed the commandments as God's standard, which we can never reach without Christ's help. We want to obey them to honor the Lord, and we try, out of gratitude and common sense, not obligation or fear.

About the same time, Phil McKown, our new pastor, noticed that our church members needed help with evangelism, so in a weekend training program, he taught us how to present the gospel. For homework, we had to go through the booklet, "The Four Spiritual Laws," with several friends.

My first subject was Becky, the least threatening of my roommates. She listened patiently until I finished. When I asked the question, "Which circle describes your life?" in other words, "Are you a Christian?" Becky said she was a Christian in good standing with God.

When we finished, I asked her opinion of the booklet. She said, "In the book of Peter it says that faith without works is dead."

"I think you mean the book of James, chapter two. And you're right. If our faith does not produce good works, it isn't faith to begin with."

Becky insisted that God's grace *can* be earned. I insisted it is a gift we don't deserve. After a few minutes, we called a truce and remained friends.

Later, Janet was in the kitchen washing dishes. I asked whether she would listen to me present my beliefs. She obliged, but a cold and distant demeanor came over her. If she agreed with something I said, she responded, "yes," or "true," and she met everything else with an icy silence. When we finished, she still said nothing. I gave her the booklet, but she left it in the kitchen until someone finally discarded it.

I wondered why she was so cold. Janet had tried for two years to convert me. Maybe hearing me explain the

Christian gospel only added to her sense of failure. I was grateful when the chill disappeared, and we were friends again a few days later.

Sharon was very sweet and listened intently as I explained the Four Laws. But she was very busy with homework, as usual, and we didn't discuss it for long.

My next prospects were the elders. Because the sixth and seventh lessons were short, the elders combined the two into one last session about the person of Jesus Christ and "our responsibility as members of the Kingdom."

One elder talked about man's need for a Savior and quoted, "for all have sinned and come short of the glory of God." He looked to the other elder for the reference, but both men had momentarily forgotten where it was found.

I said, "Romans 3:23."

Both elders, who were thumbing through their Bibles, looked up and flipped to Romans three. "You're right!" said Elder Smith in surprise. "You should be a missionary."

I couldn't resist saying, "I am one."

This last lesson, "Our responsibility as members of the Kingdom," was a final checklist before baptism. The missionaries reviewed the commandments we'd covered earlier, but now each was preceeded by, "You must. . . ." They passed quickly through this material, having resigned themselves to the fact that I was not a candidate for baptism.

When the lesson was completed, I asked hesitantly, "May I take a couple of minutes to tell you what I believe?"

I saw the elders exchange surprised glances. "I suppose so," agreed one.

I handed each of them a copy of the "Four Spiritual

Laws" and explained it step-by-step. My hands were quivering, but I kept my voice steady. I tried not to worry about what their response would be.

We came to the page in the booklet where I was to ask the reader whether his life was controlled by himself or by Christ. Both men, without hesitation, said, "My life is directed by Jesus Christ."

I realized that these elders, and all Mormons, could not be saved until they realized they were lost.

When I finished, each elder was eager to express his opinion.

"Most of this is true," said Elder Smith, "but it should be carried a step further. Faith is fine, but to obtain perfection we must follow the commandments."

"Besides that," Elder Tanner added with a grin, "they left out the restoration of the Church!"

We all laughed.

Before the missionaries left, I thanked them sincerely for giving their time and for trying to respect my beliefs. They thanked me for the dinner invitation and for being a good student.

A couple of weeks later, Elder Tanner called. As usual, he asked if there was anything he could do for me, then said he had a cassette tape he wanted to lend me. He also mentioned that Diane Cross was going to take the discussions. At first, Diane had thought taking the lessons was a bad idea, but as she heard me talk about them, she decided to take them herself. With a twinkle in his voice, Elder Tanner asked if I would like him to heat up the baptismal waters for me.

"No thanks!" I exclaimed, and we both laughed aloud.

(By the way, I don't recommend that people take these lessons unless they have had extensive experience with

Mormonism. The discussions are carefully designed to lead people into the Church, and they don't paint a complete picture of Mormonism.)

Since I'd known Janet, she had dated several men, all returned missionaries. We had talked about some of them, and often Janet wondered aloud, "Is this *The One?*" She, like all Latter-day Saint women, felt pressured to marry because the life of the Church is centered around the family. Not only that, but according to Mormon doctrine, the husband raises his wife in the resurrection.

Gary, the latest suitor, was a dashing fellow who treated Janet and all of us with elegance. Occasionally he took me for a ride on the back of his motorcycle and, more than once during the summer, he was our guest for dinner.

One night after dinner, Gary said, "I'd like to make a proposal." He pulled a diamond ring out of his pocket and slipped it on Janet's finger. We all laughed, until we realized that Gary was serious. Becky shrieked and threw her arms around Janet. Sharon sat still, with an amazed smile on her face. I sneaked out to get my camera, wanting to preserve this special moment on film.

In less than a month, now, I would be leaving Provo. I wondered whether David, my clarinet-playing friend, and I would meet again before I left.

Sure enough, one day I stepped into a elevator in the fine arts building to find myself facing him.

"Hi," we chimed in unison.

"I haven't seen you in a long time," he said.

"I'm leaving soon. I won't be back in the fall."

"Oh, I didn't know that," he said softly.

"I'm transferring to North Texas State University."

After a pause he said, "We'll miss you. Sharon will have to play twice as loud in the orchestra."

"Yeah." I smiled at the thought.

By this time the elevator had carried us to the third floor, and the door had opened. I reached out to prevent it from closing and said, "David, I'm glad I got to know you."

"Thanks Carol," he replied. "I respect you greatly, more than you know. I'm sure you'll be successful in life." He gave me a long, firm handshake. The elevator kept trying to close on my other hand.

"Bye." I stepped out slowly.

"Good-bye, Carol," he said. I watched as the door closed between us.

"Lord," I thought,"I'm glad you know what's best, when to give and when to withhold. Thank you."

As the final days of my two years in Utah grew shorter, I began to think about ways to secure the future of the Baptist Student Union. I had accumulated a volume of materials on how to lead a BSU so I organized these and other hints I'd learned in a notebook. Knowing that Dawnena, with one year of school remaining, would take my place as president, I included a special page of humorous comments for her.

Phil McKown had spoken with the BYU administrators, who had agreed to furnish a roster of the Baptist students before school began. We decided to plan a retreat before registration, and we wrote incoming students, inviting them to attend.

My mind was at ease concerning the Baptist Student Union. Who would have thought, two years ago, that we'd evangelize on campus, host a convention, enter a float in the Homecoming Parade, and become such a part of Brigham Young University that recruiters would advertise us across the nation? When I looked hard at myself, I had to say humbly, "Thank you, Lord. Your power truly is perfected in weakness."

On my last Sunday in Provo, Phil McKown invited the congregation to a fellowship after the evening service. When the group gathered in the fellowship hall, he called me forward and said, "Tonight we'd like to recognize Carol Avery. This is our time to express our appreciation for all she has meant to our congregation."

My mouth dropped open wide, and I looked at Diane and the other church members. My eyes filled with tears of love. Phil presented me with a certificate of appreciation and a Bible commentary by Matthew Henry. I was at a loss for words. Never would these people know the source of strength they had been in my life. I wished I could given them a gratitude party.

The next days passed quietly, filled with finals and packing. My father drove up from Phoenix, and we packed the car to leave Brigham Young University for the last time. Two years before, I had cried when he drove away and left me here. Now I cried at the thought of leaving BYU behind. We took a walk around the campus as the shadows lengthened and the sun turned from yellow to golden to orange. The sun was setting on a part of my life as well. I was truly sorry to say good-bye to Brigham Young University, but I knew that the school and its people would always hold a tender place in my heart. The Lord had used them to draw me closer to Him and to strengthen my faith.

Notes:
[1] In July 1986, the General Authorities announced a change in the missionary lessons. The discussions were no longer memorized word-for-word, but were presented in a more conversational style.

Epilogue

More than a decade has passed since I left BYU, and still, in the spring of 1989, the Baptist Student Union lives on. Diane Cross directed the BSU until 1982, when she went to Golden Gate Theological Seminary to teach piano and work on a Ph.D. Not long afterward, Shannon Hood, a nurse, became the volunteer BSU director. The BSU is still a BYU approved club; the students hold weekly meetings, attend conventions, and fellowship together on campus and at church.

The First Baptist Church of Provo, under the leadership of Rev. John Meador for the past ten years, baptized more new Christians than any other Southern Baptist church in all of Utah and Idaho. Now, one-third to one-half of its members are converted Mormons, including the church secretary, two of the deacons, and the Sunday School director! Wilma Meador, the pastor's wife says of their success, "We haven't been antagonistic toward the Mormons. We don't try to argue with them. John is very gentle from the pulpit. We just try to love them."

Since I graduated from North Texas State University, I have taught music, Spanish, and English in Christian and public schools in Texas, the Dominican Republic, Colorado, and China. I am now working on a Master's Degree in English at Colorado State University.

Appendix A

Witnessing to Mormons

If God has brought a Mormon friend, co-worker, neighbor, or relative into your life, you have a special opportunity to share Christ with him or her. If you accept it, your own faith and knowledge will increase, and you may even see your friend come to know Christ. Or you may not.

Don't start by witnessing to the Mormon missionaries who come to your door. They spend six days a week defending their faith. They've been instructed to spend time with people whom they can convert—not with people who are trying to convert them. As John L. Smith, director of Utah Missions, Inc., says, "When I was a vacuum cleaner salesman, I never had a woman sell me her [vacuum cleaner] while I was trying to sell her mine."[1] Besides, there's no room for doubt in a Mormon missionary's life. If he shows signs of wavering in his faith, his superiors will transfer him to another district. You won't be able to talk with him alone because he's not allowed out of sight or hearing of his companion.

Instead, befriend a Mormon you already know. Sharing Christ with a Latter-day Saint requires commitment. It may take years for a devout Mormon to come to faith in Christ. It's also easier to build a long-term relationship with someone you see regularly. In fact, "friendship evangelism" is the strategy that Mormons use to proselytize their neighbors.

Maybe a Mormon is using this strategy to proselytize you. This is an abridged version of how the program was outlined in the June 1974 issue of *Ensign,* an LDS magazine:

(1) Begin by doing minor favors for your neighbors such as babysitting, running errands, and lending tools.
(2) Selectively reveal bits of Mormon lifestyle and faith, and build friendship bonds with prospective converts before proselytizing becomes overt.
(3) Give testimonies about how happy you are in your faith, and invite your friends to Church activities.
(4) After close personal ties are built, begin to introduce Mormon beliefs.

If a Mormon is befriending you this way, the door is open for you to share your faith with him. But remember, more often than not, the Mormon succeeds in converting the Christian.

There are no guaranteed methods for sharing Christ with a Mormon. Every Latter-day Saint has different needs and different ideas. Your friend may be a returned missionary, or even a leader in the local ward, or he may be a "Jack Mormon"—the equivalent of a backslidden Christian. But the following ideas will help you as you talk with your friend.[1]

- The Bible is not a Mormon's final authority. In fact, it is the only one of their Scriptures that contains error. Before quoting much from the Bible, raise its credibility by showing archaeological evidence for its authenticity. See Josh McDowell's *Evidence that Demands a Verdict* (Here's Life Publishers), and Harry L. Ropp's *The Mormon Papers* (IVP). If a Mormon says the Bible has been mistranslated, ask him kindly and graciously for documentation.

- Mormons believe in "salvation" or exaltation by works. They expect to obtain godhood by their own efforts (although many would add sincerely, "with God's help.") The Saints have no concept of true grace. The pressure is always on them to achieve perfection. Let your friend see God's grace in your life.

- Don't underestimate your Mormon friend's intelligence,

integrity, or character. The Mormons' lifestyle—with high morals, strong family life, regular church attendance, and diligent study—puts many Christians to shame. The Mormon system appeals to the character and pride of those who do not know the Bible well.

- Mormons do not see themselves as lost. In their opinion, they not only have Christ but also the "fulness of the Restored Gospel." Share with your friend how you see yourself as a sinner. If he respects you, he may take another look at himself. Be sure he knows you respect him, too.

- Mormons teach that spiritual truth is "felt." Missionaries challenge investigators to seek "the burning in their bosom" from the Holy Ghost. Their faith is subjective. Challenge your Mormon friend to look for rational, historical proofs of his faith.

- Mormons are unaccustomed to making their own decisions about religion. They live in a strongly hierarchical structure and often expect their leaders to reason for them. Challenge Mormons to think for themselves.

- Mormons believe in "continuing revelation." The Bible (or for that matter, even their own Scripture) is not the final word. God reveals new truths to His people through the Prophet and other authorities.

- Mormons may not know the obscure, more bizarre doctrines from the early days of the Church, such as the Adam-God or the blood atonement doctrines. Don't begin with these, or with polygamy or the Negro question because new revelations have reversed these doctrines.

- Mormons use Christian words—but the meanings are extremely different from what you mean. Words such as salvation, heaven, sin, and gospel mean different things to

Mormons than to Christians. To communicate clearly with a Mormon, you must learn his language. Ask your friend what these terms mean to him.

- Don't give your friend anti-Mormon literature to read unless he asks for it. Some of this literature is inflammatory and subjective. Read it yourself and then be able to discuss the concepts with your friend.

- Mormons accept only the King James Version of the Bible. Use it in your conversations with them. Don't get sidetracked even if you like other translations better.

- Avoid talking about denominations. Mormons believe theirs is the only true Church. Emphasize a relationship with Christ, not a church.

- Share what God has been doing for you. A Mormon will be curious at daily evidence of God's power in your life.

- After you have "earned the right to be heard" with your friend, gently begin to show him some of the inconsistencies in Mormonism. Many excellent books on this subject are available. One of the most powerful tools to show a Mormon is the original (published in 1830) *Book of Mormon*. There have been approximately 4000 changes in doctrine, grammar, punctuation, and word structure since the original.

- Be bold, courageous, and forward but not aggressive or insensitive.

- As your friend opens his heart to you and to Christ, encourage him to get involved in a Bible study with you or other Christians. The Bible speaks for itself.

Living with the Latter-day Saints

- Only as the Holy Spirit removes the blinders does a person see his need for Christ. Pray. Be patient.

Your friendship with a Mormon is the most important part of your witness. If you do not genuinely love, your words will be as "sounding brass or a tinkling cymbal." Don't try to prove a point or argue doctrine—if you feel your blood pressure rising as you talk, it's time to change the subject. Mormons are great "proof-texters." If you argue, you may lose the argument. In fact, if you argue, you *have* lost the argument, because your love and gentleness are your witness.

Also, before you dump a truckload of knowledge about Mormonism on your friend, get to know him. Let him do the talking. Harry Ropp, director of Mission to Mormons, says, "As we get to know a person more intimately, we are better able to discern which information, of all the information we could give him, he most needs to hear."[2]

The best guideline I have found for witnessing to Mormons is II Timothy 2:23-26: "But refuse foolish and ignorant speculations, knowing that they produce quarrels. And the Lord's bond-servant must not be quarrelsome, but be kind to all, able to teach, patient when wronged, with gentleness correcting those who are in opposition; if perhaps God may grant them repentance leading to the knowledge of the truth, and they may come to their senses and escape from the snare of the devil, having been held captive by him to do his will."

Notes:
[1] Smith, John L., *Witnessing Effectively to Mormons,* Marlow, Oklahoma: Utah Missions Inc., 1975, page 19.
[2] Ropp, Harry L., *The Mormon Papers,* Downer's Grove, IL: InterVarsity Press, 1977, page 84.

A reprint of the 1830 edition of the *Book of Mormon* is available from the Tanners in Salt Lake City & Henry Ropp in Roy, Utah. (See "Sources of Additional Information" in Appendix C.)

Appendix B

The Bible and Mormon Doctrine

Although Mormon doctrine conflicts with the following statements, the Bible references listed support them.

1. God is spirit: John 4:24.

2. There is only one God: Deuteronomy 6:4, 32:39, Isaiah 44:6-7.

3. God is not a man: Numbers 23:19, Hosea 11:9.

4. No man can see God: Exodus 33:20, John 1:18, I Timothy 6:13-16, I John 4:12.

5. God does not change or progress: I Samuel 15:29, Malachi 3:6, James 1:17.

6. God no longer dwells in temples made with human hands: Acts 7:48, Acts 17:24, Revelation 21:22.

7. God the Father and Jesus are One (the Trinity): John 1:1-2, John 10:30, John 14:16-20, John 14:23, Philippians 2:6, Colossians 2:8-9, II Peter 1:1.

8. We are not saved by works: Romans 3:28, Galatians 2:16-3:25, Ephesians 2:8-9, Colossians 2:16-23, Titus 3:5-6.

Living with the Latter-day Saints

9. There is no second chance after death: Hebrews 9:27.

10. There is no pre-mortal existence: Genesis 2:7, Psalm 139:13-16, I Corinthians 15:46.

11. There is no marriage in heaven: Matthew 22:30, Mark 12:25, Luke 20:34-35.

12. The Bible is to be unaltered: Proverbs 30:5-6, Revelation 22:18-19.

13. Ministers of the gospel may receive compensation: I Corinthians 9:1-23.

14. Warning against angels of light (such as Moroni): II Corinthians 11:13-15.

15. Warning against another or new gospel: II Corinthians 11:4, Galatians 1:6-9, I Timothy 1:3.

The following pages contrast Mormon doctrine with the Bible. The LDS references are listed here to provide documentation of Mormon teachings. Many of the specific references are unfamiliar to Mormons. In fact, the Bible references don't prove much to Mormons, who don't accept the Bible as a final authority. The Bible, to a Mormon, is only one of four scriptures, and the only one that contains error. But if you, as a Christian, are confronted with Mormon doctrines and want to know what the Bible says about them, the references below will guide you.

There is only one God

Mormonism is polytheistic. Brigham Young said, "How many Gods there are, I do not know" *(Journal of Discourses,* Vol. VII, page 333). Joseph Smith said, "In the beginning, the head of the gods called a council of the gods; and they came together and concocted a plan to create the world and people it *(Journal of Discourses,* Vol. VI, page 5). The *Doctrine and Covenants,* one of the LDS scriptures, says, "... whether there be one God or many gods, they shall be manifest" (D & C 121:28).

In modern times this doctrine has been softened; polytheism is not in vogue. As my roommate said, *"We* have only one God. But our Heavenly Father has a God, and so on. He will always be our Heavenly Father, even when we have progressed to godhood ourselves."

The Bible teaches unequivocal monotheism.

> *"See now that I, I am He, And there is no god besides me."* —Deuteronomy 32:39

> *"... Before Me there was no God formed, And there will be none after me...Even from eternity I am He."* —Isaiah 43:10,13

> *"Thus says the Lord...'I am the first and I am the last, And there is no God besides me.'"* —Isaiah 44:6

The Trinity

Mormons abhor the doctrine of the Trinity. Joseph Smith taught, "I have always declared God to be a distinct personage, Jesus Christ a separate and distinct personage from God the Father, and the Holy Ghost a distinct personage and a Spirit: and these three constitute three distinct personages and three Gods" *(Teachings of the Prophet Joseph Smith,* p. 370).

Mormons support this belief with verses like John 20:17, in which Jesus speaks of ascending to the Father. "How," they argue, "could Jesus ascend to the Father if Jesus and God are one?" But Jesus Himself said, "I and the Father are one" (John 10:30). In John 15:26, Jesus also declares, "When the Helper comes, whom I will send to you from the Father, that is the Spirit of truth, who proceeds from the Father, He will bear witness of Me."

God is infinite, and the Trinity defies human comprehension. But the Bible calls each member of the Trinity God. The Father is God (Isaiah 64:8, John 17:1-3, I Corinthians 1:3,

I Corinthians 8:6); Jesus is God (John 1:1-2, Colossians 1:3-4, 9-15, 2:8-9, II Peter 1:1); the Holy Spirit is God (Acts 5:3-4). Each member of the Godhead is proclaimed to be God, and the Bible teaches that there is only one God. The Bible leaves us with the inescapable conclusion that the three distinct Persons must be God—and be One.

Interestingly, the Mormon scriptures themselves teach the doctrine of the Trinity. Second Nephi 31:21, in the *Book of Mormon*, says, "...And now, behold, this is the doctrine of Christ, and the only and true doctrine of the Father, and of the Son, and of the Holy Ghost, which is one God, without end. Amen." The *Doctrine and Covenants* 20:28 says, "Which Father, Son, and Holy Ghost are one God, infinite and eternal, without end. Amen."

In spite of these passages, Mormons will argue that God the Father, Jesus Christ, and the Holy Spirit are separate "personages."

God is not man

The *Doctrine and Covenants* 130:22 says. "The Father has a body of flesh and bones as tangible as man's; the Son also; but the Holy Ghost has not a body of flesh and bones, but is a personage of Spirit. Were it not so, the Holy Ghost could not dwell in us."

Latter-day Saints insist that God is an exalted man with a body of flesh and bone. They support this from Genesis 1:26-27, which states that God created man in His own image, and from Luke 24:39, where Jesus tells the disciples, '... touch Me and see, for a spirit does not have flesh and bones as you see that I have."

But the Bible says that God is spirit (John 4:24). Jesus took on human form when He came to earth (Philippians 2:6-8) and God dwelled in Him (John 14:9-10). However, it doesn't follow logically that God Himself has a body just because Jesus did while on earth nor does Scripture indicate such.

> *"For I am God and not man, the Holy One in your midst...."*
> —Hosea 11:9

Mormonism also teaches that God is eternally progressive. He was a man, is now God, and is still progressing toward higher levels of perfection. James Talmage, a Mormon apostle, wrote in *The Articles of Faith* (p. 430), "We believe in a God who is Himself progressive, whose majesty is intelligence; whose perfection consists in eternal advancement—a Being who has attained His exalted state by a path which now His children are permitted to follow...."

But the Bible says,
"And also the Glory of Israel will not lie or change His mind; for He is not a man that He should change His mind."
—I Samuel 15:29

"For I, the Lord, do not change...." —Malachi 3:6

Another key doctrine in Mormonism, related to the manhood of God, is the principle of man's eternal progression. Lorenzo Snow, one of the LDS prophets, taught, "As man is, God once was; as God is, man may become." This couplet is commonly recited by Mormons today. Joseph Smith said, "You have got to learn how to be Gods yourselves..." *(Teaching of the Prophet Joseph Smith,* p. 346).

The "man can become God" doctrine is found in the Bible, in Genesis 3:5. However, it was not God, but the serpent who said, "For God knows that in the day you eat from it your eyes will be opened, and you will be like God, knowing good and evil."

No man can see God

The Mormon Church is founded upon Joseph Smith's vision in the woods, where he said that God the Father and Jesus appeared to him and told him that all the churches were wrong, and he must join none of them.

However, repeatedly, the Bible states that no man can see God.

"But He said, 'You cannot see My face, for no man can see me and live!'" —Exodus 33:20

Living with the Latter-day Saints

"No man has seen God at any time...." —John 1:18

"God... whom no man has seen or can see...."
—I Timothy 6:13,16

"No one has beheld God at any time...."
—I John 4:12

Christ *"...is the image of the invisible God..."*
—Colossians 1:15

God does not dwell in temples

Temple work is important in Mormon practice. Marriages, sealings (permanent bondings of family members), and baptisms for the dead take place in Mormon temples. Mormons are sworn to secrecy about the sacred temple ceremonies they experience, and their most sacred worship occurs in temples.

But the Bible says that God no longer dwells in man-made temples.

"However, the Most High does not dwell in houses made by human hands...." —Acts 7:48

"The God who made the world and all things in it, since He is Lord of heaven and earth, does not dwell in temples made with hands." —Acts 17:24

Now that Jesus Christ has come, believers themselves are the temple of God:

"Do you not know that you are a temple of God, and that the Spirit of God dwells in you?" —I Corinthians 3:16

"...For we are the temple of the living God...."
—II Corinthians 6:16

There is not even a temple in heaven:

> *"And I saw no temple in it, for the Lord God, the Almighty, and the Lamb, are its temple."* —Revelation 21:22

Marriage

The importance of the Mormon temple marriage is that while a civil or Gentile marriage lasts only "till death do you part," a Mormon believes temple marriage, or Celestial marriage, lasts for all time and eternity.

The Bible teaches that marriage, wonderful as it is, is only an earthly institution.

> *"For the married woman is bound by law to her husband while he is living; but if her husband dies, she is released from the law concerning her husband."* —Romans 7:2

Jesus also made it clear that there is no marriage in heaven. The Sadducees asked him what happens if a widow remarries seven times. Jesus told them, "in the resurrection they neither marry, nor are given in marriage, but are like the angels in heaven" (Matthew 22:30, parallel passages in Mark 12:19-25 and Luke 20:27-36).

When presented with this passage, Mormons will say, "We believe that there are no weddings in heaven; we only believe that couples married here will still be married in heaven." However, the passage indicates that we will be like the angels in heaven, who are sexless, unmarried beings.

Prophets

Mormons rely heavily on revelation from their prophet. To them, the prophet is the mouthpiece of God to the entire Church. They cite Amos 3:7 in support of prophetic leadership and authority. "Surely the Lord God does nothing unless He reveals His secret counsel to His servants the prophets."

During the Old Testament era, this was largely true, and this verse was written during the Old Testament times of the prophets. But when Jesus came, He said, "The Law and the Prophets were proclaimed until John; since then the gospel of the kingdom of God is preached..." (Luke 16:16, also

Matthew 11:13). Hebrews 1:1-2 says, "God, after He spoke long ago to the fathers in the prophets in many portions and in many ways, in these last days has spoken to us in His Son...."

Mormons also quote New Testament references to apostles and prophets, namely Ephesians 2:20 and Ephesians 4:11. But as Marvin Cowan, an expert on Mormonism, says, the word "prophet" has a broad meaning of "proclaimer of God's truth" in the New Testament. And in that sense, the church today has living prophets —believers with the gift of truth-telling.[1] But as is shown by the verses above, the role played by prophets like Isaiah and Jeremiah came to an end in Jesus Christ.

Paid Clergy

Mormons are proud that their bishops (leaders of local congregations or wards) do not receive salaries. They are laymen who hold full-time jobs while leading a ward in their "leisure" time. Mormons support this by quoting I Peter 5:2, "...shepherd the flock of God among you, not under compulsion, but voluntarily, according to the will of God; and not for sordid gain, but with eagerness," and Isaiah 45:13, "...'He will build My city, and will let My exiles go free, without any payment or reward,' says the Lord of hosts."

These isolated, vague references cannot stand against I Corinthians 9:1-23, Paul's lengthy defense for Christian leaders receiving compensation for their spiritual ministry. Another clear reference is I Timothy 5:17-18:

> *"Let the elders who rule well be considered worthy of double honor, especially those who work hard at preaching and teaching. For the Scripture says, 'You shall not muzzle the ox while he is threshing' and 'The laborer is worthy of his wages'."*

Salvation

In any church, faith, or religion, salvation is a critical issue. A religion's explanation of salvation reveals its doctrine about God, man, heaven, and hell. Article Three of Joseph Smith's

Articles of Faith says, "We believe that through the Atonement of Christ, all mankind may be saved, by obedience to the laws and ordinances of the Gospel."

What Mormon writers mean by salvation is slightly clarified in *Doctrines of Salvation,* by Joseph Fielding Smith (p. 134). He says "Salvation is twofold: General—that which comes to all men irrespective of belief (in this life) in Christ—and Individual—that which man merits through his own acts through life and by obedience to the laws and ordinances of the gospel."

This "general salvation" is often equated with resurrection, and is not what Mormons are striving to obtain. Individual salvation, also called exaltation, is the goal Mormons seek. This salvation yields a place of glory in the celestial kingdom, and puts one on the path to godhood. Individual salvation "is attained by virtue of knowledge, truth, righteousness, and all true principles . . . . There is no salvation outside the Church of Jesus Christ of Latter-day Saints" (McConkie, *Mormon Doctrine,* p. 670).

Mormons do not believe in salvation by faith. Individual salvation is merited through obedience. Talmage, in his *Articles of Faith* (p. 479) says, "The sectarian dogma of justification by faith alone has exercised an influence for evil." In defense of their position, Mormons adamantly proof-text this by quoting James 2:20 (KJV), "But wilt thou know, faith without works is dead?"

The whole Bible teaches that faith without works isn't really faith. Saving faith in Christ Jesus will produce changes (i.e. good works) in a person's life, but those good works don't produce salvation. Over and over the Bible proclaims that faith, not our good works, brings us into a relationship with God.

"For we maintain that a man is justified by faith apart from works of the Law."   —Romans 3:28

"For if Abraham was justified by works, he has something to boast about; but not before God. . . . But to the one who

does not work, but believes in Him who justifies the ungodly, his faith is reckoned as righteousness." —Romans 4:2,5

"...nevertheless knowing that a man is not justified by the works of the Law but through faith in Christ Jesus, even we have believed in Christ Jesus, that we may be justified by faith in Christ, and not by the works of the Law; since by the works of the Law shall no flesh be justified."
—Galatians 2:16

"For by grace you have been saved through faith; and that not of yourselves, it is the gift of God; not as a result of works, that no one should boast." —Ephesians 2:8-9

Biblical Warnings

The Bible warns against some of the very traps Mormons have fallen into.

"I am amazed that you are so quickly deserting him who called you by the grace of Christ, for a different gospel; which is really not another..., But even though we, or an angel from heaven, should preach to you a gospel contrary to that which we have preached to you, let him be accursed." —Galatians 1:6-8

Mormons refer to their gospel as the "Restored Gospel" which is, indeed, a different gospel. Not only is it different, but according to church teaching, their gospel was brought by Moroni, an angel from heaven.

The Bible also warns against angels of light:

"For such men are false apostles, deceitful workers, disguising themselves as apostles of Christ. And no wonder, for even Satan disguises himself as an angel of light. Therefore it is not surprising if his servants also disguise themselves as servants of righteousness; whose end shall be according to their deeds." —II Corinthians 11:13-15

"If a prophet or a dreamer of dreams arises among you and gives you a sign or a wonder, and the sign or the wonder comes true, concerning which he spoke to you, saying, 'Let us go after other gods (whom you have not known) and let us serve them,' you shall not listen to the words of that prophet or that dreamer of dreams; for the Lord your God is testing you to find out if you love the Lord your God with all your heart and with all your soul." —Deuteronomy 13:1-3

Joseph Smith was known as a dreamer and claimed to be a prophet. He called people to follow after another god—a god who is an exalted man, who has a wife in heaven and a son, Jesus, who is the spirit brother of Satan. This god is not the God of the Bible.

Note:
[1] Cowan, Marvin, *Mormon Claims Answered.* Salt Lake City: Utah Christian Publications, 1975, p. 62.

I am indebted to Marvin Cowan whose extensive research directed me to many of the the primary sources listed.

MORMON WORKS CITED

McConkie, Bruce. *Doctrines of Salvation.* Salt Lake City: Bookcraft, Inc. 1954.

McConkie, Bruce. *Mormon Doctrine.* Salt Lake City: Bookcraft, Inc. 1966.

Smith, Joseph Fielding, compiler. *Teachings of the Prophet Joseph Smith.* Salt Lake City: Deseret News Press. 1958.

Talmage, James E. *A Study of the Articles of Faith,* 36th ed. Salt Lake City: The Church of Jesus Christ of Latter-day Saints. 1957.

Young, Brigham, et.al. *Journal of Discourses.* Liverpool: F.D. and S.W. Richards. 1854. Reprint ed. Salt Lake City. 1966.

Appendix C

Sources For Additional Information

If you want to learn more about Mormonism, don't rush out and take the missionary lessons. The organizations listed here publish newsletters, tracts, books, and audio-visual materials, and will gladly send you (often free) Christian materials about Mormonism.

1. Christian Research Institute
   P.O. Box 500
   San Juan Capistrano, California 92693
   (This is Walter Martin's ministry, the source of books such as *The Maze of Mormonism* and *Kingdom of the Cults*.)

2. MacGregor Ministries
   Box 73
   Balfour, British Columbia
   Canada V0G 1C0
   (or their U.S. address)
   MacGregor Ministries
   Box 591
   Point Roberts, Washington 98281
   (This ministry focuses on both Mormons and Jehovah's Witnesses.)

3. Mormonism Research Ministry
   P.O. Box 20705
   El Cajon, California 92021
   (Publishes a quarterly magazine and other materials and broadcasts a radio program in the San Diego/Orange County area.)

4. Saints Alive
   P.O. Box 1076
   Issaquah, Washington 98027
   (Formerly Ex-Mormons for Jesus, this organization publishes materials and produces films such as *The Godmakers*. They also focus on Masonry which has many parallels to Mormonism.)

5. Utah Christian Publications
   P.O. Box 21052
   Salt Lake City, Utah 84121
   (Marvin Cowan, an ex-Mormon, has done extensive research into original Mormon documents. He publishes *Mormon Claims Answered* and other materials.)

6. Utah Christian Tract Society
   P.O. Box 725
   La Mesa, California 92041
   (For many years, this organization has been publishing evangelistic tracts, testimonies of former Mormons, and a newsletter.)

7. Utah Missions, Inc.
   P.O. Box 348
   Marlow, Oklahoma 73055
   (John L. Smith, formerly a Baptist pastor in Utah, now a traveling speaker, produces books, tapes, and a newspaper.)

8. Utah Lighthouse Ministry
   P.O. Box 1884
   Salt Lake City, Utah 84110
   (Jerald and Sandra Tanner are both former Mormons; Sandra is a great-great-great-grandchild of Brigham Young. Their book, *Mormonism: Shadow or Reality,* is the most exhaustive single work on the history and errors of Mormonism.)

9. Watchman Fellowship
   P.O. Box 13251
   Arlington, Texas 76013
   (This organization has offices in several cities and actively combats many cults through materials and seminars. The Arlington office publishes a newspaper.)

Appendix D

Hierarchy of the Mormon Church

The First Presidency
The President (or Prophet)
The First Counselor
The Second Counselor

Council of the Twelve Apostles
These Twelve men, next in line to the First Presidency, form a "Traveling, Presiding High Council," as prescribed in the *Doctrine and Covenants* 107:65. Each member serves on an executive council within the Church. Several are also on the boards of directors of Mormon-owned corporations.

First Quorum of the Seventy
Some of these seventy men serve as executive directors of departments, such as the Historical, Priesthood, and Temple Departments, within the Church. Others are presidents and first counselors of geographical Area Councils of the Church throughout the world.

Living with the Latter-day Saints

Missionary Executive Council	**Priesthood Executive Council**	**Temple and Genealogical Executive Council**
Responsible for policy matters relating to preaching around the world	Responsible for policy matters relating to priesthood programs	Responsible for policy matters relating to temples and genealogy work

Area Council
Area Presidents
Regional Representatives

Stake Council
Stake Presidents
Below each of the Area Councils (headed by members of the First Quorum) are stake presidents who preside over a group of wards.
The Stake Council includes the stake priesthood executive committee, stake auxiliary leaders, stake public communications director, and other stake officers.

Ward Council
Bishops
Each local congregation, known as a ward, is led by a bishop (a lay church member) and a team of local lay leaders.